COMPUTER ANXIETY?

Instant Relief!

An Easy-to-Read Introduction
to IBM PCs, Compatibles
and Clones

Second Edition

Ken Ryan

Computer Anxiety? Instant Relief! By Ken Ryan

Order from: Castle Mountain Press, P.O. Box 190913, Anchorage, AK 99519-0913 (907) 563-6166
(Quantity Discounts Available)

Illustrations by Paul L. Benson, Jr.
Cover Design by Lori Rodgers
Edited by Laurie A. Hansen, Proof Positive Editorial Services
First Edition 1991 Second Edition 1992
Printed in the United States of America
Library of Congress Card Number: 92-071577

PCIP
Ryan, Kenneth David, 1954-
Computer anxiety, instant relief : an easy-to-read introduction to IBM PCs, compatibles and clones / Ken Ryan. -- 2nd ed.
p. cm.
Includes index.
ISBN 1-879925-05-2

1. IBM Personal Computer. 2. IBM-compatible computers. 3. Computer literacy. I. Title.

QA76.8.I2594R3 1992 004.16
QBI92-784

Read This First

Welcome to the second edition of *Computer Anxiety? Instant Relief!* I have kept it as simple as possible. Read this book and you will learn a lot about personal computers. You will become *computer literate*. You will begin to notice, all around you, people talking about their personal computers, and you will start to listen in and even understand what they are talking about!

If you are surprised by the brevity of this book, I hope that it is a happy surprise. Don't be fooled by its small size. This book will tell you everything you need to know to get started. When you have finished reading this book, you will have a very solid foundation of computer knowledge, which will allow you to communicate with other "computer literates." Even if you never lay your hands on a computer keyboard, you will benefit by having had much of the mystery of computers removed. You will no longer have those overpowering feelings of computer inadequacy. If you hear someone say, "I don't know what to do. My hard drive crashed today!" you will not only know what they are talking about, you might even respond with something like, "Surely you had a current backup?!?"

If, after reading this book, you decide to actually *buy* a computer, you will have all the knowledge necessary to make an *informed* purchasing decision. You will have the understanding and vocabulary that will allow you and your computer salesman to act as a team in deciding which computer system to buy. Later, you will no doubt find yourself confronted with more unfamiliar terms and jargon. The dictionary in the back should explain most of the arcane expressions you might encounter. When you start to run into difficulties with your operating system (everyone does, at first) send for a copy of ***DOS Rhymes With Toss*** (available soon), which is a good first step down the road to computer userhood.

Some power users will no doubt criticize this book as being incomplete and oversimplified, to which I will respond:

Thank You!
Thank You!

The KISS Principle
(K)eep (I)t (S)imple (S)weetheart

Table of Contents

Sharing the Responsibility

Imagine that you are in Paris, but you speak no French. You go into a bakery and look at all the different pastries. Which one should you buy? Unless the baker speaks a little English, enough to tell you what's inside the pastries, you may have a difficult time choosing one. In fact, even if he *is* able to explain the different pastries, it may *still* be difficult to choose one. Especially if you have never heard of any of the ingredients!

For many people, their first step into the world of personal computers is like their first step into a French bakery. Everything looks good. The "baker" is able to name the ingredients, but frustration arises when the ingredients are all things the customer has never heard of! ISA Bus? 4 Meg RAM?? 7 slots??? It might as well be French! As you can see, the salesman and the customer have some obstacles to overcome.

Suppose that you are the customer, and that you don't know *anything* about computers (not an uncommon situation). Do you really want to place *all* of your trust in *one* computer salesman? Might it not be prudent to seek an unbiased and *perhaps*

Feelings of inferiority and superiority are the same. They both come from fear.

Dr. Robert Anthony

more objective opinion? After all, just as there are a few unscrupulous bankers, lawyers and evangelists, there are also a few unscrupulous computer salesmen. Many consumers will want to protect themselves, and the best way is to be armed with *knowledge*.

Now, suppose for a minute that you are the world's most ethical computer salesman and your primary concern is not how big of a commission you can score, but rather serving your customer. As a good businessman, you realize that a happy customer will come back and buy more stuff (repeat business) and he will tell people about his positive experience (word-of-mouth advertising).

In the land of hardware and software, the salesman must be bilingual, and often must teach the customer two things. He must not only answer the question "Why this particular computer system?" He also has to teach the customer a new language that will allow him to understand the answer.

The proper role of the first-time computer buyer is that of a student. There is a lot to learn, and this book is your text. Do your homework and listen to what your teacher has to say, and your entry into the world of personal computing will be easy and painless.

I quit school in the fifth grade because of pneumonia. Not because I had it but because I couldn't spell it.

Rocky Graziano

The Very Basics

I promised this would be a book for beginners, so let's start at the beginning. What is a computer? A **COMPUTER** is an electronic machine. Computers are powerful tools which perform jobs, at the request of human beings, by means of stored instructions and information. These jobs may be as simple as 2 + 2 = 4, or as complex as guiding a spaceship to the outer reaches of the solar system. Regardless of the complexity of the job, a computer always reaches the solution by performing very simple tasks very rapidly.

IBM (International Business Machines) is the name of a company which has been a leader in the development and production of computers.

PC stands for **PERSONAL COMPUTER**. Originally, PC was used to describe a particular, early-model IBM computer, the **IBM PC**. As the years passed, *PC* came to refer to an entire family of personal computers, also known as **IBM COMPATIBLES**. *Personal computer* came to refer to any computer likely to be found on a desk top, regardless of the brand, and whether found at home or at the office. Currently, there are three major families of entry-level personal computers. They are:

1. **IBM/COMPATIBLES (PCs)**
2. **APPLE/MACINTOSH**
3. **COMMODORE/AMIGA**

This book will focus only upon IBMs, compatibles, and clones. Most of the general information, however, can be applied to all computers. For a more thorough discussion of Apples, Macintoshes, etc., see chapter three: *IBM, Macintosh or Something Else?*

There is some confusion surrounding the terms *compatible* and *clone*. In the early days of personal computing, back when *PC* was a strict reference to the IBM PC, the term *compatible* was used to refer to machines manufactured by the major competing companies, most notably, **COMPAQ**. The term *clone* was used to describe machines built by the many tiny "garage-based" outfits. Today, however, the terms have evolved and carry slightly different meanings.

Nowadays, to say that two computers are **COMPATIBLE** means simply that they will both run the same computer programs. If a computer is **100% IBM PC COMPATIBLE**, then it will run any program written for an IBM PC. **CLONE** is a term used to describe a copy of a computer design. Today, there are far more clones sold than IBM machines or Compaq machines. IBM clones accept all of the same upgrades and enhancements as IBM originals, and they are normally substantially less expensive.

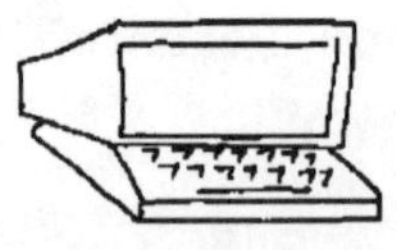

Can you spot the clones?

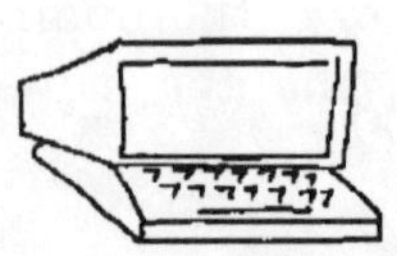

IBM, Macintosh or Something Else?

This book deals almost exclusively with IBM and compatible personal computers. There is one main reason for that decision: *simplicity*. The beginner's task would be far more complex if we were to attempt to cover all of the different computing platforms. **PLATFORM**, in its broadest definition, refers to the family, or genre of computer. Different computing platforms have their own peculiarities, and to include them all would complicate this book more than is necessary. But why have I chosen IBM compatibles (PCs)?

Earlier, I said that there are three families of personal computers. It is up to the reader to choose one over the others. The author recognizes that there is some anxiety over making such basic decisions, so let's look at some numbers. As of this printing, an overwhelming majority (roughly 80 million) computer users have chosen to purchase IBM and compatible personal computers. This compares with roughly five or six million Macintosh computers. More persuasion: a recent Gallup poll, commissioned by *Computer Reseller News*, found that on *average*, 91 percent of the desk top computers found in surveyed Fortune 1000 companies were IBM or IBM compatible computers. By contrast, only 4 percent were Macintosh computers.

The reader can rest assured that when it comes to computers, there is indeed strength in numbers. Case in point: Clones and Macs. There are a great number of clone manufacturers. There is one Macintosh manufacturer. Because of the great number of PC clone manufacturers, competition is fierce and therefore prices are lower. Much lower. The result is that IBM clones offer a far greater computing value than any other personal computer system.

Another reason for joining the big family of IBM and compatibles is to be where the software is. Because there are so many IBM users, no other system even approaches the variety of software available for IBM compatibles.

It was once a well known fact that the Macintosh computer was easier to learn and use than an IBM compatible computer. It was also true that for graphics applications, things were possible on a Mac that were impossible on a PC. Things have changed. Over the years, the Macintosh has gotten more complex and IBM compatibles have worked hard to become more "user friendly." Today the gap between the two has narrowed to the point where ease of use is no longer much of a reason to choose one system over the other. And, while Macintosh still holds a narrow lead in graphics capabilities, PC clones are rapidly closing in, and may soon dominate this field as well.

Now don't get me wrong. All of this is not to say that there is anything wrong with Macintosh or that they are inferior or even that they are fading away. To the contrary, there is not a more loyal or enthusiastic group of personal computer users than Mac users. Also, the same Gallup survey that indicated that on average, only 4 percent of Fortune 1000 desk top computers are Macs, also indicated that Macintosh usage is *increasing*. It's just that *I* recommend an IBM clone for the two reasons stated: number of users and dollar value. *You* may be one of the small percentage that choose to compute on an Apple Macintosh.

Now, you are probably asking yourself, "Didn't I read in the paper that IBM and Apple had joined forces? Doesn't that make the PC v Mac question irrelevant?" The answer is, "No." Or, perhaps, "Not yet." It is far too early to tell where this alliance will lead and what its impact will be on the personal computer industry.

APPLE + IBM = ?

The AMIGA is another fine personal computer, but it is not one that I can recommend. While it is true that Amiga offers enhanced audio and video performance at a relatively low cost, once again IBM clones have closed the gap. Most importantly, a much smaller user base means less software and less support.

Hardware and Software

All of the components of your computer system can be classified into one of two categories: hardware or software.

Anything tangible, anything you can hold in your hand, is **HARDWARE**. The keyboard, and all its little parts and pieces, the monitor, and that ominous box called the system unit, and all the mysterious components within it, are all considered hardware. If you can touch it, it is hardware.

There are lots of different components that make up your computer system. There are RAM chips and ROM chips, CPUs and coprocessors, extended memory and expanded memory, hard drives and floppy drives, motherboards and expansion boards, serial ports and parallel ports, and peripheral devices galore.

Right now, these terms may not mean much to you. You can probably tell, just by the name, that all of these strange new words represent things.

Remember, if it is a thing, then you can touch it, and if you can touch it, then it is hardware.

If you can touch it, it is hardware.

Before you have finished this book, you will understand the function of all of these hardware components. We begin by showing the three primary hardware components of any personal computer: monitor, keyboard, and system unit.

Software is something different. You cannot touch it! **SOFTWARE** is information. This information is recorded onto hardware such as floppy disks. When you buy software, you are in reality buying both hardware and software. The hardware is the floppy disk, and the software is the ***information*** recorded on the floppy disk.

A very rough analogy could be made using a musical record. In terms of hardware and software, the record and the record player would be the hardware. The software would be the music itself.

Everything your computer does is guided by software. Without software, your computer is just a useless pile of hardware. Software is divided into two broad categories: systems software and applications software.

SYSTEMS SOFTWARE is the information your computer needs to get itself up and running, and to maintain itself. Take that useless pile of hardware we call a computer and add systems software, and suddenly it becomes smart enough to accept applications software.

When you get up in the morning, you probably use the bathroom, take a shower, brush your teeth and perhaps have a cup of coffee or tea. Your computer also needs to do certain things when it wakes up. Because your computer is so dumb, it must be told over and over again, the things that it needs to do, just to start up and keep going. It must not only be told to brush its teeth, it must also be told where the toothbrush is located. The set of instructions that supply the computer with this basic information is the systems software.

APPLICATIONS SOFTWARE is information the computer uses in order to accomplish specific tasks, or solve specific problems under the direction of you, the user. Add some applications software, such as a word processing program, and your computer becomes a high-tech typewriter capable of truly incredible editing feats. Similarly, other applications software allow the computer to perform complex mathematical computations (spreadsheet programs) or manage large collections of information (database programs). Other applications software might allow you to figure your taxes, balance your checkbook or even book your airline tickets.

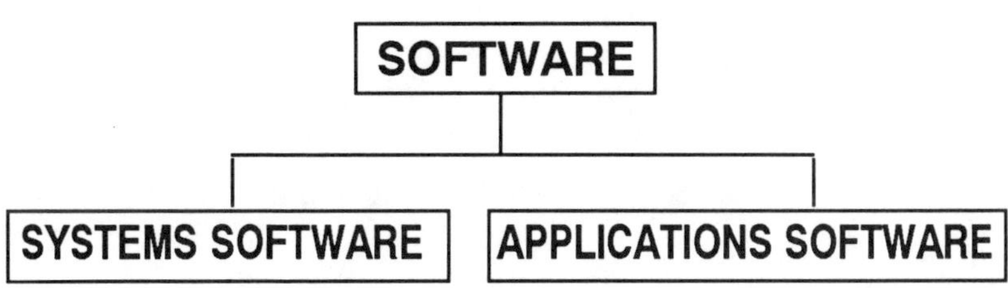

Another word for software is **COMPUTER PROGRAM**. Later in this book, we will discuss some of these computer programs in greater detail. For now, just think of software as information. This information acts as instructions for the computer. Some of these instructions are essential. These are the systems software and the computer must always have them. Others are optional. These are the applications software and they are dependent upon the specific task the computer is asked to perform.

If you can only cuss at it, it must be software.

Bits, Bytes and More

The whole world seems to be composed of opposites. Hot and cold. Light and dark. Wet and dry. Yin and Yang. Either/Or. The computer world is no exception. In fact, this concept of opposites constitutes the very foundation upon which the computer operates.

Computers are not very smart. Essentially, all they are capable of understanding is one very basic concept. Something can be "*either*" this "*or*" that. Let's look more closely at this either/or system of logic.

Computers don't speak English or French or Spanish, but rather they use an entirely different system of communication called a binary system. For now, it is sufficient if you simply understand that a **BINARY SYSTEM** reduces all letters, numbers, and other characters to combinations of two symbols.

In Morse Code, the most famous binary language, those two symbols are "*dots*" and "*dashes.*" The famous signal, SOS, is composed of three dots, followed by three dashes, followed by three more dots. Morse code uses two symbols, dots and dashes, to represent all of the letters of the alphabet. In a similar fashion, computers use a binary code (ones and zeroes instead of dots and dashes) to represent each of the letters on the keyboard. This method seems cumbersome to humans, but it is very handy for a computer.

Remember, a computer is an electronic machine. It uses pulses of electrical current to get the job done. Just as we have eyes which are capable of sensing whether a light bulb is "*on*" or "*off,*" a computer is capable of sensing whether there is a pulse of electricity, or no pulse. If there *is* a pulse, the computer interprets that as a one, and if there *is not* a pulse, the computer interprets that as a zero.

In human language, such as English, the most fundamental units are the letters A, B, C . . . Z. In the language of mathematics, the fundamental units are the digits, namely 0, 1, 2 . . . 9. In the realm of computers, there are only two fundamental units: **ONE** and **ZERO**. We call these two basic symbols **BITS**. The name "*bit*" is a shortened version of the term "**B**inary Dig**IT**."

A **BYTE** is merely a chunk consisting of eight bits. A byte is used to represent one character (one letter, number, etc.) The figure on the following page illustrates how all of the letters of the alphabet can be represented by a binary system using only two fundamental symbols. In the case of Morse Code, it's easy. The letters are simply represented by various combinations of dots (.) and dashes (—).

In the case of computers, it's not quite that easy, and a couple of extra steps are involved. First, the letters are assigned their own unique number. It is important that everyone use the same procedure when assigning numbers to stand for letters, so that computers and programmers can talk to each other without getting confused. For instance, if one programmer used the number 12 to stand for the letter "G," and another programmer used the number 12 to stand for the letter "j," you can see where there could be some confusion. To promote harmony, a standard was adopted that decided once and for all what numbers to assign to the different symbols, in this case, letters. This standard is called **ASCII** (American Standard Code for Information Interchange). Pronounce this "**askee**."

Once a letter has been assigned a number, it must then be converted to base two. Remember, our computer is very stupid. All it is capable of is deciding that something is "**either**" this "**or**" that. Our ordinary, everyday math uses base ten, which has ten different symbols (0, 1, 2, 3, 4, 5, 6, 7, 8, 9). It is far too complex for our computer. Base two, on the other hand, is a special math that has only two symbols, ones and zeroes. That's just what we are looking for. If our computer is capable of determining that something is either this (1) or that (0), then it can also figure out that [01000001] (65 converted to base two) stands for the letter "A." As a computer *user*, you don't have any need to know how to convert from base ten to binary (base two). All you need to understand is that your computer uses combinations of only two symbols, and that each one of those symbols is called a bit.

LETTER	MORSE CODE	ASCII	ASCII CONVERTED TO BINARY
A	.-	65	01000001
B	-...	66	01000010
C	-.-.	67	01000011
D	-..	68	01000100

Do you see that [01000011] [01000001] [01000010] = CAB?

Now that you understand bits and bytes, this next subject should be easy. If you spend any time at all hanging out around an office water cooler, you have probably heard mention of kilobytes (**K** or **KB**) and megabytes (**M**, **MB**, or **MEG**).

A **KILOBYTE** is simply 1024 bytes. A **MEGABYTE** is another word for 1024 kilobytes (which also equals 1024 X 1024 bytes or 1,048,576 bytes). To put these terms in perspective, the text in a single page of typing takes up about 2K. A megabyte can hold about 500 pages of typing. A **GIGABYTE** is 1024 megabytes, or 1,073,741,824 bytes. Over two thousand 250-page novels can fit into one gigabyte.

BIT = 1 or 0
BYTE = EIGHT BITS (01000010)
KILOBYTE = 1024 BYTES
MEGABYTE = 1,048,576 BYTES
GIGABYTE = 1,073,741,824 BYTES

Twenty five novels might consume 10 megabytes of storage space.

Why is a kilobyte 1024 bytes, rather than 1000 bytes? And why is a megabyte 1024 kilobytes, rather than 1000 kilobytes? Remember, since computers speak a binary language, they like the number *two*. 1024 is simply two raised to the tenth power.

Floppy Disks and Drives

Imagine a filing cabinet. Now imagine a big room full of filing cabinets. Go ahead, open one of the drawers. See how full it is? Try another. There certainly are a lot of documents stored in each full drawer, aren't there? Imagine a drawer with about 750 double-spaced pages of text. This is approximately equivalent to the storage capacity of a single 3 1/2" **FLOPPY DISK**! Kind of boggles the mind, doesn't it?

Floppy disks, like filing cabinets, are **STORAGE DEVICES**. They are one of the places where the computer can store information, and they come in two sizes: 3 1/2 inch and 5 1/4 inch. Each of these sizes comes in two models: standard and deluxe. The only thing that makes a deluxe better than a standard is that the deluxe diskette will hold substantially more information than the standard diskette.

For example, you can buy a standard 3 1/2" floppy, and it will store 720 kilobytes of information, or you can buy a deluxe 3 1/2" floppy that will store twice that amount, or 1.44 megabytes. To the human eye, they appear identical. To the computer, they are very different. The same situation exists for the 5 1/4" floppies. *Standard and deluxe* (360K and 1.2MB).

Of course this is all too easy to understand, so rather than calling these different capacity disks "*standard*" and "*deluxe*," the jargon committee chose two very confusing names. They decided to call the standard version "**DOUBLE-SIDED/DOUBLE-DENSITY**," and the deluxe version "**DOUBLE-SIDED/HIGH DENSITY**." To make things even more difficult, they abbreviate them DS/DD and DS/HD. Are you confused yet?

Try this: The smaller (3 1/2") disks store more information than their big brothers, the 5 1/4" disks. Figure that one out! Now, let's make things even more muddled. Not only can you buy a double-sided/double-density 3 1/2" floppy which stores 720K and a double-sided/high-density 3 1/2" floppy which stores 1.4MB, you can also buy a double-sided/high-density 3 1/2" floppy which is labeled as storing 2 megabytes, but in reality, it only stores 1.4 megabytes! If you are still not confused, throw this book away and get one on brain surgery. You are much too smart to be messing around with computers!

	3 1/2 inch	5 1/4 inch
STANDARD (DS/DD)	720K	360K
DELUXE (DS/HD)	1.44MB	1.2MB

FLOPPY DISK STORAGE CAPACITY

Notice that the *larger* size (5 1/4") floppy actually holds *less* than the *smaller* size (3 1/2").

Obviously, we need to have some method for putting information onto these floppies, and for reading back information already stored there. For each size (3 1/2" or 5 1/4") disk that your computer will accept, there is a corresponding **DISK DRIVE**. These disk drives are normally located inside the system unit, although they are sometimes separate pieces of equipment. Some systems have both a 3 1/2" and a 5 1/4" drive, while other systems will only have one size or the other.

Usually a disk drive which will run the deluxe disks will also run the standard ones. The reverse, however, is not true. Many drives will run only the standard disks.

An important part of the disk drive is the **READ/WRITE HEAD**. The floppy disks have a magnetic coating on them, much like cassette tape or VCR tape. The read/write heads are capable of reading or writing binary information to or from the floppies in a fashion also similar to the tape player or VCR.

Another thing you should know about floppies is that they can be **WRITE PROTECTED**. This means that they are protected from being erased or written over. This is accomplished in different ways, depending on whether one wants to protect the 3 1/2" or a 5 1/4" disk. The 5 1/4" disk has a small notch along one edge. To protect the disk, simply cover this notch with one of the sticky tabs that comes with it. (The sticky tab resembles a miniature mailing label.)

Floppy disks, like audio cassettes, can be used over and over again. With a little bit of care, they can last a long time.

It is even easier to protect the smaller 3 1/2" disks. These floppies have a small hole in one corner with a cover that slides back and forth. If the cover is positioned so that you can see through the hole, the disk is protected. Slide the cover to the other position where you can no longer see through the hole, and you can now write to the disk.

Floppy disks are sensitive in a number of ways. Avoid folding them or creasing them in any way. You need to be especially careful when mailing them. Put them in a box or, at the very least, encase them with stiff cardboard.

Don't allow the disks to get excessively cold or hot. This means don't leave them in the sunlight, where they might soak up the heat from the sun. Also, don't leave them in your car when it's cold outside. You can run into real problems if you bring cold disks into a warm house, and condensation forms on the disk, and then you insert the wet disk into your computer.

Beware of magnetic fields! These invisible hooligans can erase or scramble your data. They can be found around such innocent-looking devices as televisions, telephones, digital watches, radios, speakers, and even your computer monitor. Also, keep the disks away from X-Rays. (X-Ray machines produce powerful magnetic fields.) Dust can also be a problem. Keep your disks in some sort of storage box with a lid. Don't attempt to clean the surface of the disk, and never force a disk into a disk drive.

Try to fill out the label before you put it on the floppy disk. If you must write on a label which is already affixed to the disk, lightly use a felt tip pen to avoid possible damage caused by pressing with a pencil or ballpoint pen.

It is possible to buy floppy disks that are "pre-formatted," but normally this is something that the user does himself.

To FORMAT a floppy disk, the computer essentially "draws lines" that divide the floppy disk into sectors and tracks. SECTORS divide the floppy the way a pie is divided when cut into equal size pieces. TRACKS are concentric lines, like the lines formed when a pebble is dropped into a pond.

The computer does this to make it easier to store and locate data on the disk. It's like when you are looking for a town on a roadmap. By consulting the index, you can narrow down the area that you need to search.

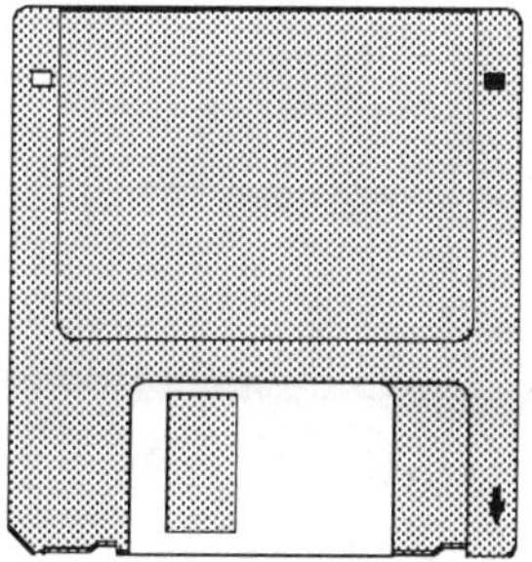

3 1/2" FLOPPY DISK

5 1/4" FLOPPY DISK

Now available. . .
SUPER FLOPPIES!

There are great new things happening to floppy disks. Toshiba America has developed a version of the 3 1/2" size that uses a special barium ferrite coating, giving the disks a capacity of 2.88MB. Brier Technology has released its Flextra 25MB drive. More of these "super floppies" are sure to follow.

Hard Disks and Drives

There is a small stack of platters inside the system unit. This stack of platters is called your **HARD DISK**. Because this disk is normally mounted permanently inside the system unit, it is often called the **FIXED DISK.** Hard disks have much in common with their cousins, floppy disks. Both are storage devices for binary information. They both operate in a similar fashion. They use pulses of electricity to affect the magnetic coating on the surface of the disk.

A hard disk is capable of storing much more information than a floppy disk. An average priced computer one might find in a home or small business will probably have a 40-to-60 megabyte hard disk. Larger and larger hard disks are becoming more and more common. In fact, it is not at all uncommon for PCs to have hard disks capable of storing 100 MB, and even more.

In addition to holding lots of information, a computer can locate information stored on its hard disk much faster than if it were stored on a floppy. The period of time required to find information stored on the hard disk is called the **ACCESS TIME**, and it is measured in thousandths of a second, or milliseconds (**ms**). Obviously, a faster access time is an advantage.

The hard disk also has a corresponding disk drive, including read/write heads. In the case of the hard drive, these heads are located **very, very close** to the hard disk itself. It would be catastrophic to the data on the hard disk if these read/write heads were to actually contact the surface of the disk. For this reason, it is important that you **PARK** the hard disk drive before moving the system unit. This is done quite simply by typing a command which causes the read/write heads to move to a position where the hard disk will not be damaged if the system were to receive a sudden jolt. Many newer hard disks are self-parking, and automatically park themselves when not in use.

When considering what size hard disk to buy, remember this: sometimes, bigger **is** better. Conventional wisdom says to figure out how much storage space you will need - and DOUBLE IT! Dollar for dollar, hard disks are incredibly good buys.

There are several types of hard drives, all of them good, but currently the best price/performance award goes to a design known as IDE (integrated drive electronics).

IDE hard drives offer access times of less than 13ms, data transfer rates of 1.5 MB per second and require a mere 4 watts of electricity. Something better is sure to come along, but right now, for most beginners, IDE is probably the best choice.

CD-ROM

There is now a new combination disk/disk drive that represents a major technological advance over the hard disks and floppy disks that we have already discussed. This new technology is called **CD-ROM (COMPACT DISK-READ ONLY MEMORY)**.

Instead of using a magnetic coating and read/write heads, CD-ROM uses a laser to detect the binary information stored on the disk. The disk itself looks just like the audio CD which has captured the music world, and the disk drive looks much like a portable audio CD player. In fact, most CD-ROM drives actually double as audio CD players.

As the name implies, the computer can read information which is stored on these compact disks, but it cannot write information onto them (actually this technology *is* available and is called **REWRITABLE OPTICAL**, but it is still too expensive for everyday folks). The big advantage of compact disks is the amount of information that can be stored on them. A single compact disk can hold *hundreds of megabytes* of information (up to 650MB).

Compact disks are also more durable than floppy disks. They are not affected by magnetic fields and they are far less subject to deterioration caused by environmental factors such as dust, humidity, etc. They hold an advantage over hard disks in that they are portable and easily transported from one computer system to another (like from home to office).

When you start using a computer, if you become involved in computer graphics, you will quickly appreciate the value of a high-capacity storage medium such as the compact disk. A normal size page (8½" x 11") filled with graphics will consume a full megabyte of storage space. Add color to that image and you can multiply the storage requirement many times over.

Many people want to have a whole library of such images to enhance their documents and presentations. You can see that it would be easy to fill a hard disk with graphics images.

Another use for compact disks is to allow persons to own personal reference libraries. CDs can practically store such things as encyclopedias, dictionaries, almanacs, telephone directories, complete works of Shakespeare, all the issues of the *New York Times* for a particular year, etc.

The performance of the disk drives themselves can be measured in a couple of ways. We already discussed one of these, access time (the time required to find a particular random piece of information stored on a disk). Currently, CD-ROMs are considered fast if they have an access time of 300ms.

Another measurement of CD-ROM performance is **DATA TRANSFER RATE**. This is a measurement of how much information a CD-ROM can feed back to the PC in a particular time period. Currently, a data transfer rate of 150K (150 Kilobytes per second) is considered good.

CD-ROMs can be either internal or external, meaning that they can be installed inside your system unit (as are floppy drives and hard drives, normally) or they can be separate pieces of equipment, joined to the system unit with a cable. The obvious advantage of the internal drive is that it doesn't take up any extra desk space. Internal drives also cost about $100 less than the comparable external drive.

A single compact disk can hold the equivalent of 275,000 typed pages of text.

Before we launch into this next subject, let me remind you that our purpose right now is not to become instant computer technicians. Rather, we are building a foundation from which we can explore all of the intricacies and subtleties of computers ***IF WE CHOOSE.*** *Enough said. Let's get back to work.*

Memory

Memory is also a form of storage, but it's not the filing cabinet type of storage like the floppy disks and hard disks discussed previously.

COMPUTER **MEMORY** STORES INFORMATION THAT THE COMPUTER NEEDS FOR THE JOB IT IS WORKING ON.

If we think of floppy disks and hard disks as being like filing cabinets, then we might think of memory as being like a desk top. If we had a particular job to do at the office, we might take files out of the filing cabinet and put them on our desk top. It is in this manner that the computer removes information from a floppy disk or hard disk, and temporarily stores them in memory.

Remember, computer memory stores information that the computer needs for the job it is working on!

There are two kinds of memory with which we must familiarize ourselves. You may have heard of them: ROM and RAM. Usually, when we speak of computer memory, we are speaking of RAM.

RAM stands for **RANDOM ACCESS MEMORY.** The first thing you need to know about RAM is that when you turn the computer off, it vanishes, or more accurately, any information stored in RAM vanishes. Because RAM relies upon the electrical power of the computer, and the fact that it erases itself when that power is interrupted, we say that RAM is **VOLATILE.**

RAM is measured in Kilobytes or Megabytes. It used to be very common for an average PC to have 640 kilobytes of RAM. Nowadays, it is common for PCs to have two full megabytes of RAM. It is desirable to have four megabytes, or more.

To better understand RAM, let's imagine we are going to write a letter using our word processing software. First, we tell our PC we want to use the word processing program. The computer will then go to the spot where the word processing program is stored (probably the hard disk) and make a copy of the essential parts of the program, which it temporarily stores in RAM. When this happens, we say that the computer **LOADS** the program.

Remember, RAM stores information the computer needs to accomplish the specific task it is working on. Since we are going to write a letter, the computer must have access to the word processing program.

Next, we begin typing our letter. As we type away and create our document, it is all being stored in RAM. Finally, when we are finished, we store the letter to either a floppy disk or the hard disk. When we do this, we say that we **SAVE** the document. If we did not save the document, it would vanish when we turned off our machine (remember, RAM is volatile).

Suppose that later we want to add to the letter, or modify it in some way. We can simply load a copy of it into RAM, and now we are free to manipulate it in any fashion we choose. When we finish this time, we have the option of replacing the old letter with the new one, or we may want to save this new letter alongside the original letter.

Obviously, it makes a difference how much RAM your computer has. Each piece of software requires a certain amount of RAM.

Your computer must have at least that much RAM to operate the program, plus some more RAM to hold the job you are working on. Some jobs require much more RAM than others. It is a good thing to know what kind of jobs you are going to do, and the RAM requirements of those jobs. That way, you can better match your future computer to the jobs it will be asked to perform.

Most PCs come with a certain amount of RAM as "standard equipment," with the option of adding more either at the time of purchase, or at a later date. If you are thinking of buying a computer, you will want to know how much RAM comes as standard equipment and how much can be added later. Find out how much it will cost to add RAM, and whether or not you can perform the upgrade yourself.

Remember, the more RAM your computer has, the bigger the job it is capable of performing. Think of RAM as the "*working memory*" of your computer. If you are going to be working with graphics, you need a lot more RAM than if you are only going to be doing word processing.

ROM stands for **READ ONLY MEMORY.** Whereas RAM **CHIPS** are like blank sheets of paper, waiting for information to be written to them, ROM chips already contain instructions permanently etched into them.

Unlike RAM, ROM does not rely upon an outside power source. It is always there, and it never changes. Because it is self-sustaining, we refer to ROM as being **NON-VOLATILE.**

Whenever you turn on your computer, the first thing it does is find ROM and execute the instructions that are permanently stored there. Later, we will talk some more about what those instructions are. For now, just think of ROM as being permanent and never changing, and realize it is inaccessible to you, the user.

Think of floppy disks and hard disks as being like filing cabinets, and think of RAM as being like your desktop.

Two terms you are certain to encounter are EXTENDED MEMORY and EXPANDED MEMORY. Let's try to break through the technobabble and explain what you need to know about these two terms.

Briefly, IBM compatibles have an inherent problem using RAM, and to use more than 1MB requires a special system. Both extended and expanded memory refer to memory in excess of 1MB. The primary difference between the two lies in the design of the special system that the computer uses to access that memory.

So, which one do you want? Very probably you will want extended memory, because this is the kind that works with the very popular operating system, WINDOWS (see page 59).

Processors

The **CPU** is the **CENTRAL PROCESSING UNIT**, or brain of the computer. Often called simply "processors," these **MICROCHIPS** are located inside the system unit. It is the processor that carries out the instructions of the software. Here is a list of the most common CPUs that are found in PCs.

8086
80286
80386
80486

Processors just keep getting better and better. That is, they continue to improve in their ability to process more and more information, and in their ability to do it faster and faster. In this list, the slowest comes first and the fastest comes last. The primary developer and manufacturer of these processors is a company called **INTEL**.

It might help to think of these processors as engines. Just as a bigger engine means a faster car, a faster processor means more work being performed in the same amount of time.

The 80286, 80386, and 80486 are normally referred to as simply 286, 386, and 486.

There is another factor affecting the ability of a computer to process information, and that is the speed at which the CPU operates. This speed is measured in **MEGAHERTZ**, or millions of cycles per second, commonly abbreviated **Mhz**. Normally, a computer with a 286 processor set to run at 16 Mhz will be faster than one with the same processor set to run at 12 Mhz.

Some processors can operate at two different speeds. These **TURBO** chips can run either "slow" or "fast." Why would you want your processor to run more slowly? Well, some computer programs (not many) won't work properly at the faster speed.

In addition to the central processor, some computers have a **MATH COPROCESSOR**. This is a specialized processor which only performs mathematical computations. While the coprocessor is busy solving complex math problems, the main processor is free to perform other chores.

Usually, a coprocessor does not come as standard equipment, but may be added as an option. Bear in mind, some computers are incapable of accepting a coprocessor. If you want the capability of adding a coprocessor, look for a computer that comes with a **COPROCESSOR SOCKET**. This means that there is a place inside the computer where you can plug in a coprocessor, if you decide you need one. In the case of the 486 processor, the coprocessor is already built-in.

Coprocessors are numbered in a fashion similar to main processors, and the two must be properly matched. A computer with an 80286 CPU would require an 8028**7** coprocessor. An 80386 must be matched with an 8038**7** coprocessor. In addition, both the CPU and the coprocessor must run at the same speed. If the CPU runs at 16 Mhz, the coprocessor must also run at 16 Mhz.

Coprocessors are of no value for such tasks as word processing, but they can greatly improve performance on math related jobs such as spreadsheet calculations. Other applications where coprocessors can show their stuff are the fields of computer graphics and computer aided design.

We speak of one CPU as being a **16 BIT PROCESSOR** and another CPU as being a **32 BIT PROCESSOR**. These terms refer to the amount of information that can be "processed." Processing refers to two separate functions: first, what takes place *inside* the CPU, and second, the *transfer of data* from the

CPU to memory and other components. This transfer of information takes place along a **DATA PATH**. The wider the data path, the greater its ability to carry information. Think of the data path as a freeway, and think of the bits of information as the automobiles. Obviously, a 32-lane freeway can handle more traffic than a 16-lane freeway. The same is true for data paths. When the CPU can process 32 bits of data at a time, and the data path can handle the same amount, we have a 32 bit computer. Both the 80386 and the 80486 are 32 bit processors. The 80286 and the 8086 are 16 bit processors.

But what if the CPU is capable of working with 32 bits of information, but it is connected to the rest of the computer with a 16 lane freeway? When this situation exists, we refer to the system as a 386SX.

The latest development concerning CPUs and personal computers concerns *upgradable* CPUs. Intel has devised a system that will allow users to purchase a 486 CPU and then later purchase a special chip that will double the CPUs clock speed.

These upgradable 486 CPUs are expected to be the processor of choice very soon.

What is a computer *chip*? Back in the olden days (prior to 1947), complex electrical circuits functioned by using vacuum tubes. These devices were quite large and required lots of power. Worse yet, they were unreliable. The more complex the circuit, the more vacuum tubes needed. The more vacuum tubes, the greater the odds of one malfunctioning. The result: computers based on vacuum tube technology were very large and very unreliable.

In 1947, along came the transistor. Transistors were great. They could do what vacuum tubes did, and they could do it reliably, while consuming far less power. They were also much smaller than vacuum tubes. There was still one problem. To build the complex circuits necessary for even simple computing, thousands and thousands of transistors were required, and it was difficult to wire them all together. Engineers struggled along with this second generation of transistor-based computers until a new technology was born.

That technology was the microprocessor, or computer chip. Scientists discovered how to take a sliver of semi-conducting material, such as silicon, and etch a circuit onto it. Portions of the circuit are treated chemically, and the result is a complete electronic circuit that will perform the function of millions of vacuum tubes or transistors, and all of the wiring needed to hold them together. Microchips are very small, very reliable, and very easy to mass produce.

Motherboards and Other Boards

True to form, the jargon committee stayed late the night they cast their blessings on our next subject. This component is so important, they decided to give it at least **four different names!**

Whether you call it the system board, planar board, logic board, or the **MOTHERBOARD**, it is the single largest component inside the system unit.

If you were to remove the cover from the system unit, the one component most likely to first catch your eye would be the motherboard. It is that large printed circuit board which covers the entire bottom of the system unit. Its function is to hold and connect many of the vital electronic components that make up the basic computer system.

There is a socket to plug in the CPU, and usually there is another socket for an optional math coprocessor. Remember back when we talked about ROM and RAM? ROM and RAM come to the computer in the form of small computer chips. The motherboard has sockets for these guys, too. There is also a socket for the "clock" chip. This is the one that sets the pace for the computer. (Remember our discussion of processor speed?)

Built into the motherboard are sockets called **EXPANSION SLOTS**, into which one can plug additional, smaller circuit boards called **EXPANSION BOARDS** (also called daughter boards, enhancement boards, adapter boards, add-in boards, option boards). These boards are also referred to as **CARDS**, as in expansion card, enhancement card, etc.

The function of these expansion boards, or expansion cards, is to give the machine a degree of flexibility. For instance, you may decide that you want more RAM, but your motherboard is completely full. You might buy an expansion board and plug it into one of the slots on the motherboard, and thus you would have the RAM that you needed. Or you might decide that you want the ability to import graphic images into your document. To do this, you would need a scanner. A scanner requires additional hardware that is not found on your basic computer. That's why it comes with an expansion board. Maybe you have run out of space on your hard disk. One option would be to install a hard card. This is a special expansion board designed to act like another hard disk. They are available in capacities ranging from 50 to 100 megabytes, or more.

There are many other uses for expansion boards. A few are: modem boards, FAX boards, video boards, audio boards, etc. This ability to allow for future expansion is referred to as **OPEN ARCHITECTURE.**

Monitors

The jargon committee's finest hour came the night that they addressed the subject of monitors. Now, it is all a matter of record. EGA, VGA, SUPER VGA, CGA, MDA, MCGA, 640 x 200, 720 x 400, CRT, VDT, LCD, pixel, palette, and on and on and on.

First, what is a monitor? A **MONITOR** is that TV-like object that sits on top of the computer. The monitor is the means by which the computer communicates with you, the user. Thus we refer to it as an **OUTPUT DEVICE**. The monitor works hand in hand with another piece of equipment, the **VIDEO CONTROLLER**.

The video controller is located inside the system unit, along with a lot of other electronic goodies. The video controller and the monitor must be compatible with one another. Not all video controllers will run all monitors.

Sometimes the video controller is built right into the motherboard. Often, it comes as an expansion board, and is plugged into an expansion slot in the motherboard. Today's software puts a much higher demand on the video system, and older systems with outdated video controllers can take a comparatively long time to "redraw" a screen. Nowadays, it is quite common for someone to upgrade their video controller by installing a **VIDEO ACCELERATOR BOARD**.

The flashing marker which appears on the screen is called the CURSOR. The cursor marks the spot where the computer will place the next character.

Monitors come in different sizes, and until recently the most common sizes were a 13" or 14" (diagonal) screen. The latest software will work fine on a 13" or 14" screen, but a larger screen is preferable, with 15-inchers rapidly becoming the standard. It may not sound like much, but a 15-inch diagonal screen, with its improved technology, will have approximately 35% more area than an older 13.5-inch model.

Like a TV, a monitor can be either color, or non-color. Some software require a color monitor, most do not. In addition to color capability, monitors also offer varying degrees of **RESOLUTION**. Resolution is a measure of the clarity of the picture on the screen.

The picture that shows up on the computer screen is actually made up of tiny dots of light called **PIXELS** (short for "picture element"). Monitors are graded according to how many pixels they are capable of displaying. A monitor rated at 640 x 480 pixels will have a clearer image than one rated at 640 x 200 pixels. The greater the number of pixels, the greater the resolution, which means the picture is sharper.

If you go away and leave your computer monitor turned on for an extended period of time, there is a possibility that the image on the screen will "burn" itself into the screen, resulting in a permanent shadow image. To prevent this, programmers have written software that continually change what appears on the screen when it is not in use.

If you see fish swimming across the screen devouring one another, or flying toasters, or kaleidoscopic images, you are probably watching a SCREEN SAVER in action.

If you decide to opt for the less expensive **MONOCHROME** monitor, be aware that you are not necessarily restricted to black and white. Monochrome refers to "one-color." The most popular one-color alternatives are the green or the amber screen.

High Resolution

Typically, PC packages come with monochrome monitors as standard equipment. Just as you might opt for a leather interior when purchasing a new car, you can opt for a higher quality monitor when you buy your computer. Nowadays, almost everyone buys a color VGA monitor.

There is one final consideration when choosing a monitor. You need to make certain that the monitor you buy will display graphics, as well as text. There are still some text-only monitors floating around out there, and you don't want to get stuck with one. Today's software demands graphics capability. Graphics-capable monitors are available in both color and monochrome.

Whichever monitor you decide on, proper care will include regular cleaning with a non-abrasive cleaner. It is also a good idea to keep it under a dust cover when it is not turned on. You will also take special care to never use the dust cover when the monitor is turned on. It will overheat and self-destruct, and might even start a fire.

Low Resolution

Keyboards!

Keyboards

The **KEYBOARD** is the piece of equipment normally used to give information to the computer and to issue it commands. Thus, we say the keyboard is an **INPUT DEVICE**.

Most keyboards have adjustable legs which allow the keyboard to be used laying flat, or tilted slightly. Also, there is usually a pencil ledge above the top row of keys. All of the IBM-style keyboards feature a typewriter-like arrangement of alphabet keys **(ASDF JKL;)**, plus additional keys not found on a typewriter. Different manufacturers place these keys in slightly different locations, depending upon the taste of the designer.

The **ARROW KEYS** allow you to move the cursor around the screen. Usually, they are located on the **NUMERIC KEYPAD**. The numeric keypad makes it easier to type in numbers. There is a special key called the **NUMLOCK** (number lock) which is used to choose between the numeric keypad or the arrow keys. The **FUNCTION KEYS** are used to send instructions to the software. They do different things, depending on the software being used. The function keys are used alone or in conjunction with the **CTRL**, **SHIFT**, or **ALT** keys (control, shift and alternate). Thus, each function key is capable of sending at least four separate commands to the software program.

For example, with WordPerfect, F2 by itself issues the "forward search" command. Hold down Shift and press F2 and you issue the "backward search" command. Holding down the Alt key and pressing F2 yields the "replace" command, and holding down the Ctrl key while pressing F2 gives the "spell" command. If you are using a different word processing program, then the function keys have entirely different meanings. Some software also use a combination of the Ctrl, Shift, and Alt keys in conjunction with the function keys, offering even more possibilities (Ctrl/Alt F1, etc.).

Some other special keys normally found on IBM style keyboards are: escape, backspace, home, page up, page down, insert, delete, and print screen.

There are three basic types of keyboards in the IBM world. The first keyboard to emerge was the 83-key keyboard. There were two big problems with its design. One problem concerned toggle keys. A **TOGGLE KEY** is a keyboard button which, when pressed, activates a particular feature and, when pressed a second time, deactivates that same feature. The most common toggle key is the numlock key. On the original keyboards, there was no indicator to tell the user whether or not the key was engaged.

A second and more serious problem was that the shift key had been moved from the place where it was normally located on standard typewriters. Typists revolted, and IBM responded with its improved 84-key keyboard. Indicator lights were added for the toggle keys, and the shift key was moved back to its historic placement. The 84th key was the "system request" key. Unless you use your PC as a terminal hooked up to a large (mainframe) computer, you won't use the system request key.

Nowadays, most PCs come with the 101-key/enhanced keyboard. This keyboard includes a separate numeric keypad, which makes working with numbers much simpler.

There is a very special key on PC clone keyboards called the "BACKSLASH" (\ ) key. When you start learning how to use a computer, it will become apparent just how important this key is.

For now, just be aware that it is completely different from, and not to be confused with the "forward slash" (/) key. Because it is so important, it is usually placed well away from the standard alphabet keys, making it hard to strike by mistake.

Printers

The **PRINTER**, like the monitor, is an output device. It transfers information from the computer to sheets of paper. There are a number of different types of printers available, and they each have advantages and disadvantages.

DAISY WHEEL

The daisy wheel printer closely resembles a typewriter. It has a little wheel with all of the letters and numbers embossed on fingers around the outside. The wheel strikes the ribbon once for each character, just like a typewriter. Daisy wheels do an outstanding job of printing **LETTER QUALITY** text (equal to that produced by a good typewriter), but they have one major drawback; they have no graphics capability. Even simple charts and graphs are beyond the reach of the daisy wheel. Other less serious drawbacks are that they are noisy and the slowest of the printers (which is still pretty fast when compared to most human typists).

DOT MATRIX

The dot matrix is the most popular printer around today, and for very good reason. They are fast, inexpensive, and they can print text which is **NEAR LETTER QUALITY**, or practically as good as that produced on a typewriter. Also, they can print graphics. The way they operate is by using a series of pins to create tiny dots on the paper. These dots can be arranged to form a letter, a line, or some other graphic depiction. The more pins the printer has, the greater the quality of the print. The typical high quality dot matrix printer uses 24 pins. Less expensive dot matrix printers are available which use only 8 or 9 pins. Both daisy wheel and dot matrix printers are **IMPACT PRINTERS**, and therefore they are suitable for use with duplicate forms that use pressure sensitive carbon paper.

LASER

The laser printer is the latest development in printers. Laser printers work like photocopiers in that they use **TONER** (tiny solid particles) instead of ink. A drum rotates inside the printer. Guided by the computer, a laser draws a magnetic picture of the page to be printed onto the drum. The drum passes through the toner, and the toner sticks to the magnetized areas. The toner is then transferred and bonded to the paper. Until recently, laser printers were big and expensive. Now, however, they are small enough to fit on your desk, and they are inexpensive enough to be a viable option for home and small business use. They are fast, very quiet, and the quality is superb.

INK JET

The ink jet printer actually shoots ink right onto the paper through tiny nozzles. Some ink jets can print several different colors on the same page. They are very quiet and can be quite small. Their print quality is also very good.

PLOTTER

A plotter can be used for text, but it is really designed to create drawings. There is a little hand which holds one or more pens, which is then guided over the paper. Small table top models are used for charts and graphs, while larger floor models are used for engineering applications.

If you magnify the impression created by a laser printer, you will see that it is actually made up of tiny dots. The quality of output of laser printers is measured by the number of DOTS PER INCH (DPI) that make up the impression. Typically, 300 dpi has been the standard. Recently, advances have been made, allowing for 600 dpi and even 1000 dpi output from relatively inexpensive laser printers.

Peripheral Devices

PERIPHERAL EQUIPMENT is hardware which plugs into the motherboard, often through sockets, or **PORTS**, on the back of the system unit. Think of these ports as doorways to the motherboard. The basic peripherals needed to use your system are a monitor, floppy drive, and keyboard. Other peripherals we have already discussed are hard drives, CD-ROMs and printers.

Each peripheral device will have a corresponding **CONTROLLER**, which can be built into either the motherboard or the peripheral device itself, or it can be a separate component (expansion board) which plugs into an expansion slot. These controllers allow the CPU and the peripheral device to communicate, or **INTERFACE**. The two most common interfaces found on PCs are the **PARALLEL INTERFACE** and the **SERIAL INTERFACE**. Depending upon the type of interface, the device connects to the PC through a **PARALLEL PORT** or a **SERIAL PORT**.

The most common use for the parallel interface is to connect the computer to a printer. A bundle of individual wires is connected to the printer at one end and the computer at the other. One entire byte of information is transmitted at a time. This is accomplished by sending eight bits down eight separate wires (remember, there are eight bits in a byte) in one pulse.

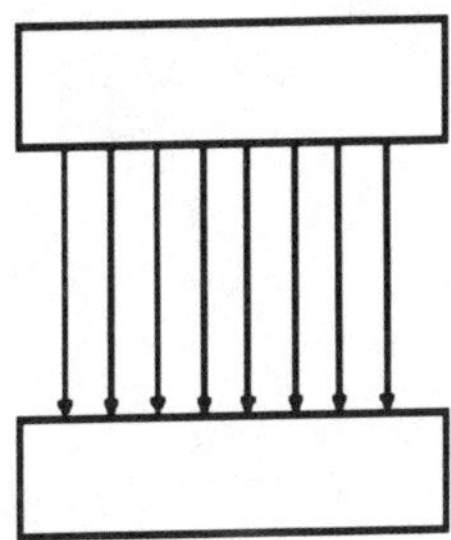

A parallel interface sends one complete byte (8 bits) of information, as a single pulse, down eight different wires.

When the printer receives a complete byte, it notifies the computer by sending a message on a ninth wire, called the **ACKNOWLEDGE LINE**. Other wires are reserved for other special signals. These special communications lines are called **HANDSHAKE LINES**. **HANDSHAKING** is the successful communication between a computer and a peripheral device.

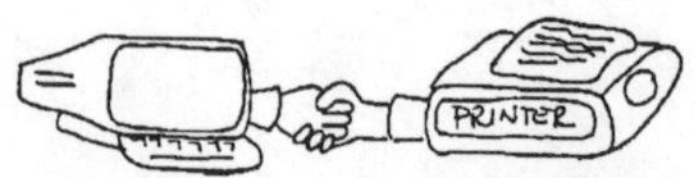

The second type of interface is the serial interface, also called an **RS-232**. Using this system, data is transmitted bit by bit, single file, over a single wire. A second wire is used to send information the other direction, and a third wire acts as a ground.

The resulting continuous stream of bits can make it difficult for the equipment to discern which bits go together to make up a byte. To alleviate this problem, bytes are sent as part of a **DATA FRAME**. This means that in addition to the eight bits that make up the byte, additional bits are sent with it to allow the computer to distinguish when one byte ends, and the next byte begins. Thus, a single byte of information may require up to 12 bits being sent.

The speed at which a serial interface transmits information is measured in bits per second **(BPS)**. Common speeds for data transmission are 1200, 2400 and 4800 bits per second. To put this in perspective, 2400 bits per second is approximately equal to 200 bytes, or about 40 words per second.

A serial interface sends multiple bits of information, one after another, down a single wire.

MOUSE

The mouse is another peripheral device. It gets its name from a mouse-like appearance. With its small body and long tail, the mouse is used as a pointer, giving the user an easy way to move the cursor around the screen. There are two basic types of mice: mechanical and optical.

Mechanical mice have a steel ball in the bottom of the mouse body. The ball protrudes from the "belly" of the mouse, and it turns as the mouse is moved about the desk. There are sensors which translate the movement of the ball into cursor movement. Optical mice are similar to their brothers, the mechanical mice. The difference is that an optical mouse uses lights and sensors and a special reflective mouse pad. It has no moving parts.

Different mice have different resolutions. A mouse with high resolution doesn't have to be moved as far as a mouse with lower resolution, in order to accomplish the same cursor movement on the screen.

TRACKBALL

A trackball does the same thing as the mouse. It acts as an input device, allowing the user a convenient method for moving the cursor about the screen. Unlike the mouse, the trackball is stationary. Cursor movement is achieved by rotating a ball with one's thumb. The advantage to the trackball is that it uses less desk space than a conventional mouse.

SCANNER

Scanners are devices which translate visual information into digital information. Copies of pictures and drawings can be stored as a file in digital form. Text may also be scanned. Remember, though, scanners "take pictures," they do not "read." Sophisticated software can, however, carefully examine a picture of text and look for patterns that represent letters, and thus the computer **can** actually "read." This ability to translate shapes to letters is called **OPTICAL CHARACTER RECOGNITION**.

There are two types of scanners: **FLATBED** and **HANDHELD**. With a flatbed scanner, the page to be scanned is placed under a lamp-like affair, which automatically scans the page. A handheld scanner must be dragged over the page. Previously, flatbed scanners could scan a larger area (a handheld scanner is only about four inches wide, a flatbed is 10 - 14 inches wide). Today, software exists that can stitch together the images scanned with a handheld model, so that now the handheld can actually scan a larger image than the flatbed.

MODEM

Modems are devices used to transmit and receive information from one computer to another over normal telephone lines. Modems are both input and output devices. The name comes from the words **MO**dulation and **DEM**odulation. These are terms used to describe the conversion of information from digital to analog, and from analog back to digital.

Digital is the code the computer understands, and analog is the code the telephone understands. The modem on the transmitting computer takes digital information and converts it to analog, and then feeds it to the phone lines. The modem on the receiving computer receives the analog signals, converts them back to digital, and then feeds them to the computer.

Modems are rated according to their speed. This rating is expressed as either **BAUD** or

The terms BAUD and BPS both describe the speed at which data is transmitted. BPS simply stands for "bits per second." It means exactly what you would think that it means: the speed at which data is transmitted, as measured in the number of bits per second. BAUD is a very technical term that has to do with the shape of the electrical impulse which is carrying the information. All you really need to know is that baud rate and bps are nearly identical. You can think of them as being the same thing.

BPS (BITS PER SECOND). Currently, the most common modems found attached to personal computers are rated at 2400 bps. More and more are starting to use 9600 bps modems.

When talking about computers, we always seem to come back to the compatibility issue. This is especially true when talking about modems. After all, the whole purpose of a modem is to communicate with another PC, so it is natural to expect that they would need to have certain things in common. These commonalities, necessary for successful communication between two modems, are called **STANDARDS**.

Rest assured that the jargon committee has cast great favor on this field of personal computing. There is CCITT V.32 and V.32bis. And V.42 and V.42bis. And MNP 4 and MNP 5. Is any of this important? Yes! It's all important, but not necessarily to you, the beginner.

For more information on V.32, V.32bis, V.42, V.42bis, MNP 4 and MNP 5 look them up in the dictionary in the back.

If you are considering a modem, allow me to make the following recommendations: accept no less than a 2400 bps modem that supports MNP 4 and MNP 5, even better would be a 9600 bps modem that supports V.32, V.42 and V.42bis. If you want a thorough explanation of what all this stuff means, go to the bookstore and get one of those big, thick computer books that cost about thirty bucks and weigh about twenty pounds. You're certain to find a detailed discussion, but I doubt if you'll really understand it (*I* don't). Keep in mind that you can get a FAX-MODEM that will not only act as a typical modem, it will also send and receive FAXES.

TAPE BACKUP

No system of storing information is infallible, and your hard disk is no exception. In fact, it is not a matter of ***if*** your hard disk will fail. It is a question of ***when***. Because he knows that sooner or later something will happen to his data, the prudent person will always keep a current **BACKUP COPY** of anything important. Many people make their backup on floppy disks, but this can be quite time consuming. You have to sit at the computer, alternately removing and inserting floppy disks, at the command of the computer.

```
INSERT BACKUP DISKETTE 01 IN DRIVE A:
PRESS ANY KEY WHEN READY
```

(Wait for the computer to copy the information to the floppy disk.)

```
INSERT BACKUP DISKETTE 02 IN DRIVE A:
PRESS ANY KEY WHEN READY
```

(Wait for the computer to copy the information to the floppy disk.)

```
INSERT BACKUP DISKETTE 03 IN DRIVE A:
PRESS ANY KEY WHEN READY
```

(Wait for the computer to copy the information to the floppy disk.)

```
INSERT BACKUP DISKETTE 04 IN DRIVE A:
PRESS ANY KEY WHEN READY
```

This can be quite a time consuming process if you have a lot of data to back up. Tape backup provides an alternative. Instead backing up to a whole series of floppy disks, you can copy the information onto one micro-cassette. There is no need to sit in front of the computer and oversee the operation. Just tell the computer what to do, and then let it do it!

DOS

You have probably heard the term **DOS (DISK OPERATING SYSTEM)**. At this point, you don't need to know very much about DOS. If you decide to become a user, then it will be necessary to learn the basics of DOS. You can do so quite easily and painlessly by getting a copy of ***DOS Rhymes With Toss*** (available soon).

For now, be content with a simple explanation of what DOS is. DOS is a computer program. It allows the computer to be smart. Smart enough to know how to store information on a disk, and find it again. Smart enough to obey your commands and the commands of the various software programs.

You might think of DOS as a host, insuring that you, your computer hardware and your software mingle properly. Or perhaps a traffic cop, working to avoid "gridlock." Better yet, think of DOS as a manager — the one who helps all of the players on the team work together smoothly.

DOS comes in different versions. The higher the number, the more improved and advanced the program. For instance, DOS 4.01 is a more advanced version than DOS 3.3. DOS version 5 is currently the latest release. If two versions of DOS carry numbers that are only slightly different, that means that only slight changes were made. For instance, there is a DOS version 4.0 and a DOS version 4.01. The numbers are only slightly different, so we would expect the differences to be slight.

The different versions of DOS become important when you start buying software. Certain programs require that your computer use at least a certain version of DOS. For instance, WordPerfect 5.1, the latest version of a very popular word processing program, requires DOS 2.0 or later versions.

DOS is the manager.

Way back in 1981, when IBM introduced the original IBM PC, they needed an operating system. Rumor has it that IBM approached Digital Research, the dominant company in the field of operating systems, to see what they could come up with, but Digital was less than enthusiastic about having IBM as a customer. There was, however, another company ready to fill the order.

Microsoft, headed up by Bill Gates, rose to the occasion and provided IBM with the operating system they needed. Microsoft also reserved the right to sell the program to other computer manufacturers. Thus, we have PC DOS and MS DOS. PC DOS is the version used by IBM, and MS DOS is the version used by everyone else.

Windows

MICROSOFT WINDOWS is a computer program which creates a graphical environment that sits between the user and DOS. If the computer is running only DOS, the user is confronted with a blank screen and must know what command to type in. On the other hand, if the computer has Microsoft Windows in addition to DOS, the computer screen comes alive and offers the user choices, by way of icons.

ICONS are simply small pictures which stand for a particular command. For example, there is a little picture of a clock, and you use this icon to prompt your computer into telling you what time it is. Another icon has the shape of a printer. This one is used to access the print manager. This aspect of Windows which uses icons to issue commands is referred to as a **GRAPHICAL USER INTERFACE (GUI)**. (Pronounce this "**GOOEY**.") It is the same type of system that earned its popularity on the Apple Macintosh.

Perhaps just as important as the graphical aspect of this interface is the fact that it is *consistent* from one software program to another. In other words, when you have learned one Windows program, you can sit down with another Windows program that you have never seen before, and it will look very familiar. It is much easier to learn to use new programs in the Windows environment than in the pure DOS environment. This feature is very attractive to businesses, whose employees don't become productive until they become proficient.

Windows is much more than a GUI, however. One other thing that Windows does is allow the computer to run multiple programs simultaneously. If you are running plain vanilla DOS, to switch from your word processing program to your database program requires that you exit out of word processing, and then enter into the database. Windows handles this situation much more elegantly.

With Windows, each program is assigned to its own portion of the computer screen. Each of these separate portions of the screen is called a window. Now, let's look at the above situation in the Windows environment.

You are running your word processing program, and you want to go to your database. The first thing you would do would be to shrink the window that contains the word processing program. You might shrink it down to where it occupies one quarter of the screen, or you might shrink it all the way down to where it is merely represented by an icon. Now, you can enter your database.

You open this program in its own separate window, which you expand to cover almost the full screen while you are working on it. Meanwhile, the word processing program is still running "in the background." If you want to go back to the word processing program, just shrink the database window, and expand the word processing window. This ability to run more than one program at the same time is called **MULTITASKING**.

Now let's assume that both the word processing program and the database programs are versions written especially for Windows. If this is the case, they may be linked in a very special way, through something called a **DYNAMIC DATA EXCHANGE (DDE).** The DDE allows you to tag certain information so that when it is changed in one application, it automatically changes in other applications.

In the above example, you may have been writing a business letter with a table listing your current inventory when suddenly your assistant came in with the latest, up-to-date inventory report. You could update your database with the latest numbers, and the table in the letter would automatically be updated as well!

There is much more that Windows does for you and your computer. So much more that it requires a separate book to adequately cover the subject.

PC, XT, AT

As you wend your way down the road of IBM and IBM compatibles, you will undoubtedly run across terms such as **PC COMPATIBLE,** and **PC XT COMPATIBLE**. These terms are used to compare IBM clones to original IBM equipment. To make sense of them, let's look at a little PC history.

Once upon a time, in the middle 1970s, two guys named Steve built a home computer in a garage. Later, they started selling them. Then, they started making lots of money. They called their computer Apple.

Big, corporate IBM recognized that there was a large fortune to be made selling computers to small businesses. They organized a special team to develop a "personal computer," and sent them to Boca Raton, Florida, where they could work in peace.

In August of 1981, IBM announced the **PC**. This machine was a huge and instant success for IBM in the personal computer marketplace. The PC was built around the 8088 processor, and came with a standard 64K RAM. In March of 1982 IBM announced the **PC XT** (*Extended Technology*). This was also based on the 8088 processor, but added a hard disk.

In August of 1984 came the **PC AT** (*Advanced Technology*). This machine had the much more powerful 80286 processor, and ran about 8 times as fast as the original PC. Things remained relatively stable for the next few years. The PC AT remained the standard. Different models were released, and the last one introduced the very popular 101-key enhanced keyboard. Clones appeared in great numbers, far outselling their IBM look-alikes.

Later, the much more powerful 32 bit processor, the Intel 80386, was released and was very successful, gradually replacing the AT as the personal computer of choice.

When a company calls their clone an "AT," or says it is "AT Compatible," they are contending that their machine is roughly equivalent to the IBM counterpart. That is, it has the same features, is built around the same processor, and will run the same software as an IBM AT.

Since the XT and AT, even more powerful processors have been produced (80386 and 80486). Computers built around these processor run 20 - 40 times as fast as the original PC.

In April of 1987, IBM made some big changes in the design of their computers, making them much more difficult to copy. IBM also became much more fervent in protecting the rights to their new design. They called their new computer the Personal System Two, or **PS/2**. The new design was called **MICRO CHANNEL ARCHITECTURE**, or **MCA**. IBM offered the technology to clone manufacturers, for a fee.

Unwilling to pay IBM for the right to copy their new design, the other major computer companies collaborated to design their own alternative to MCA. They called it **EXTENDED INDUSTRY STANDARD ARCHITECTURE**, or **EISA**.

Over the years, IBM's share of the personal computer market has dwindled. They are no longer the Goliath of the industry. Gone are the days when IBM set the standard, with others following their lead. What will be IBM's role in the personal computer marketplace in the 1990s? What effect will their alliance with Apple Computer have? Time will tell.

Portable Computers

Portable computers are currently the fastest growing sector of the personal computer marketplace. Great strides are being made, resulting in products which are smaller, lighter, more powerful, and less expensive.

One way to classify computers is by their size. If they are the size of a briefcase, or a small suitcase, they are called **LUGGABLES or TRANSPORTABLES.** Luggables are all but disappearing because newer technologies today allow smaller machines to do the things that yesterday could only be done by luggables.

The next smaller class of portable computer is called **LAPTOP**. Laptops are considerably smaller than luggables. They are small enough, in fact, to rest comfortably on one's lap. It is more common to see them perched on airline trays and nestled away in cafe booths.

Take a laptop, and shrink it just a little bit, so that it is approximately the size of a small three-ring binder, and it qualifies as a **NOTEBOOK** computer. Notebooks are becoming very, very popular.

Laptop and notebook computers are available in a wide variety of configurations. Some use the 8086 processor, however it is becoming more and more common to find them equipped with the more powerful 286 and 386 microprocessors. 486 notebooks have just recently come on the scene. Some only have hard drives, some only floppies. Still others have both. The portable computers of today may have as little as 640K of RAM, or as much as 32MB. The screen may be CGA, EGA or VGA. There are even color displays available, and the price of these is finally starting to come down.

A few portables will only operate off of normal house current, however most will also come with a rechargeable battery pack. These battery packs may last from 1 - 4 hours between recharges. Recharge time might vary from 1 1/2 - 6 hours. Also, most portables will offer an "auto-adapter" option, which enables the computer to run off of your car's 12-volt current.

There is one final class of portable computers. These are machines which easily fit in the palm of one's hand. Quite logically, they are called **HAND HELD COMPUTERS, or PALMTOPS**. Because of their size, their keyboards are too small to allow for true "touch-typing," and their screens are naturally limited as to the amount of information they can display. These limitations notwithstanding, palmtops are remarkable machines, and are now available as true MS DOS computers. Some of them will run for weeks or even months off of a few regular AA batteries. They even come with cables and special software that makes transferring information to a desk-top computer quite simple.

A concept that seems to be becoming more popular is that of the **DOCKING STATION**. In this scenario, one might have a laptop computer and two docking stations - one at home and one at work. The laptop has the processor, RAM and a hard drive. The docking stations might have a full size monitor and keyboard, a couple of floppy drives, a bigger hard disk, and a bunch of expansion slots to allow for system expansion. This setup makes it very easy to compute at home, at work and on the road.

Software Revisited

The computer cannot do anything without first being given instructions. These instructions must be extremely explicit. You cannot simply say, "Take out the trash." You must say something more like,

"Johnny, I am talking to you."
"Find trash."
"Pick up trash."
"TRASHDOOR." (This would tell the computer to follow a separate set of instructions which describe in great detail how to find the door.)
"Open door."
"Go outside."
"Close door."
"TRASHOUT." (This would tell the computer to follow a separate set of instructions which describe in great detail where to put the trash and how to get back to the door.)
"Open door."
"Go inside."
"Close door."
"Go to room."

These very explicit instructions, which are so painstakingly simple, are called computer programs. Computer programs are called software.

Many people believe that in order to utilize a computer, it is necessary to know how to program a computer. Nothing could be further from the truth. There are expert computer programmers who are happy to do that for you. No, to utilize a computer, it is not necessary that you know anything at all about computer programming. What **is** necessary is that you learn how to operate the software these wizards create.

As noted earlier, there are two broad classes of software: systems software and applications software. Systems software consists of programs the computer needs to get itself up and running, and to maintain itself. Some of these programs are stored on a disk (your hard disk, if you have one) and some are permanently etched onto computer chips and stored as ROM (read only memory).

ROM contains some very basic programs. These instructions include start-up routines, as well as programs to manage the computer hardware. Because of their unique function, and because ROM is actually a hardware component, we sometimes refer to the programs stored in ROM as **FIRMWARE**.

Applications software consists of computer programs which we, the users, utilize to perform specific tasks. Some of the most common applications for personal computers are: word processing, spreadsheet manipulations, database management, desktop publishing, educational uses and telecommunications.

WORD PROCESSING

Load the proper software into your computer and suddenly you have an amazing machine that can put an ordinary typewriter to shame. On-screen corrections are a breeze. No more white-out, worn out erasers, or angry restarts.

The "block" feature, found in most moderately sophisticated word processing programs, will allow you to isolate whole blocks of text and manipulate that block by deleting it, moving it or even adding it to a different document.

You can forget about spelling errors if your word processing program has a built-in dictionary. This program will automatically check each and every word in the document, and if it finds an error, it will present you with properly spelled choices which most closely resemble the misspelled word.

Suppose you are writing a letter, and you realize you have just used the word "direct" for the third time in the same paragraph. With a built in thesaurus, you can simply move the cursor to the word "direct," strike the correct function key, and PRESTO! you are presented with alternative words such as: aim, focus, head, point, steer, conduct, guide, lead, address, apply, bend, devote, command, instruct, order, administrate, control, govern, manage, and regulate.

Perhaps you are writing a lengthy paper about classical musicians, and you learn something about Beethoven which you want to include. Rather than paging through the document until you finally stumble upon the section talking about Beethoven, you could instead institute a search. Just as the software can look for misspelled words, it can also search for any pattern of letters that you choose, in this case, "Beethoven." In the blink of an eye, the cursor will move to the first occurrence of the word.

Popular word processing programs of the day include: WordPerfect, Microsoft Word, Wordstar, Professional Write, Displaywrite and Ami Pro.

DESKTOP PUBLISHING

Start with a plain old document, add graphics, different styles of type, complex page design, etc., and you begin to move out of the arena of word processing, and into the wonderful world of desktop publishing. Popular desktop publishing programs of the day include: Pagemaker, Ventura, PFS: First Publisher, Publish It! and Microsoft Publisher.

SPREADSHEETS

One very important business application for the personal computer is in the manipulation of spreadsheets. Spreadsheets are used to answer the all-important question "What If?"

"What if gross sales increase by 4%, while fixed expenses increase by 2.8%? What if the cost of goods increases by 6%, while retail prices are raised by 8%, and gross sales decrease by 2.2%? What if salaries are increased by 5%? What if this year's growth is equal to last year's growth?"

Knowing the answers to questions such as these can help managers with their decision making chores, and a PC with spreadsheet can perform all of the complex mathematical computations and provide the answer. Best of all, they can do it swiftly and accurately. Today's spreadsheet software include: Quattro Pro, Lotus 1-2-3 and Microsoft Excel.

DATABASES

A database is a collection of information. A simple example of a database would be a mailing list. Database management programs allow one to access very specific portions of very large collections of information. These large collections of information are broken into categories called **FIELDS**.

Suppose, for example, you are the secretary of Ken's Komputer Klub. Further suppose this is a nationwide club with millions of members. Each time a person joins the club, he fills out an information sheet which includes data such as his address, phone number, the type of computer he owns, the town where he lives, and his specific computer interests. Each of these categories (address, phone number, type computer, etc.) is a different field. Once this information is entered into the database, it can be accessed in any number of ways, according to the field. Example: You could ask for a list of the names and addresses of all members living in Cleveland who own IBM compatibles and are interested in desktop publishing. Or, you could ask for a list of all members who own 386 machines and whose phone number has an area code falling between 614 and 722.

Some of today's database programs are: Paradox, dBase IV, rBase and Foxpro.

Similarly wonderful things can be done in other areas by using different applications programs to perform different tasks. Educational software can teach you how to type or allow you to learn a foreign language. Inventories can be kept continuously up to date. Mailing lists can be managed almost effortlessly. Repetitive invoices can be printed automatically. There is almost no end to the practical ***applications*** of your computer.

Software is normally copyrighted and it must be registered to one owner. It is not nice (read: illegal) to copy someone else's software. The two exceptions to this are shareware and public domain software.

PUBLIC DOMAIN is a term for software which can be freely copied and used, without restriction.

SHAREWARE is very similar to Public Domain. The difference is that shareware authors request that users send them a donation if they benefit from their product.

Shareware and public domain programs exist for all of the more common applications, such as word processing, spreadsheets and databases. Typically, shareware programs are not as sophisticated or powerful as their commercial counterparts. They are, however, often perfectly adequate.

Telecommunications

TELECOMMUNICATION is the process of using a modem to allow two or more computers to communicate with one another over ordinary telephone lines. In addition to a computer and a modem, to telecommunicate you also need **TELECOMMUNICATIONS SOFTWARE**. These computer programs range from simple to sophisticated. Simple shareware programs are available for a few dollars and high-end communications packages can cost several hundred. It is not uncommon to get software bundled with your modem when you buy it.

When two computers telecommunicate, they may do so directly, with one computer dialing directly to the other. It is far more likely that two computers will telecommunicate indirectly, by calling a host computer. This host computer is often referred to as a **BBS** (bulletin board service). There are thousands of little BBSs all over the world. There are also a few really big ones. The big ones include CompuServe, GEnie, Prodigy and America Online. There are now a great number of reasons why one might want to contact a BBS. Some of them are:

E-MAIL

Electronic mail (E-Mail) is like a private message service. You have an electronic "mailbox," into which people can send you messages. You are the only one who can read what's in your mailbox, with the exception of the **SysOp** (system operator).

FORUMS

These are like roundtable conferences of people with a common interest. Forums are gatherings around an electronic fireplace, giant free-for-all public debates, limited only by the subject of the particular forum. Forums exist for every conceivable subject. Whether you are interested in politics, travel or sports (or hundreds of other topics), there is a forum for you.

TECH SUPPORT

Tech(nical) support is the process of one person helping another to solve his or her hardware or software problems. Computer people really enjoy helping others, and entire forums are dedicated to this purpose. Indeed, some large software manufacturers include in their instruction manual a particular forum or E-Mailbox number to contact for help.

SHOPPING

Yes, Virginia. There is an electronic mall.

SHAREWARE

Some BBS have gigantic hard disks that are just crammed full of shareware. There are two things to keep in mind when copying this "free" software: you may be paying by the minute for the time it takes to download and if you decide to keep and use the shareware, you are expected to pay the author.

DATABASES

With a computer, a modem, and telecommunications software, you have whole reference libraries literally at your fingertips. Browse through *all* the daily newspapers, check the Associated Press for the latest news, search reference books, go to the law library, etc. Best of all, you can search by subject. For instance, you might want to search all Alaskan newspapers for articles about grizzly bears.

Buying Your First PC

What to Buy

If you have decided it is time to purchase a PC, you will need to expand your horizons a bit. Go to the newsstand and purchase copies of at least three of the many computer magazines. Avoid those geared exclusively for the other types of computers (Apple, Macintosh, Commodore, Amiga, etc.) and instead search for ones that are geared toward IBM compatibles in general. Look for the ones that have the most advertising. Now that you know something (quite a bit, actually) about computers, you will actually understand some of what is written.

Take these magazines home and spend some time looking at the advertisements. The ads are frequently more heavily concentrated toward the back of the magazine. You will notice there are a multitude of companies and that many offer package deals that include at least a system unit, a monitor and a keyboard. Some of them include printers, most do not.

Don't worry about reading and understanding the articles. You are still in kindergarten, and most of the articles will be written on at least a junior high or high school level. Studying the ads in these magazines will inform you as to the many brands that are available, what constitutes a "typical" package, and what a **FAIR** price might be.

If you want to go one step further, go to the library and look through back issues of many of the computer magazines. ***Read only those articles which evaluate PCs.*** Do not be alarmed if you do not understand everything written in the article. It is not necessary to be a computer whiz to buy your first system.

When doing comparisons, keep in mind the primary considerations are: 1) What is the microprocessor (CPU)? 2) How much RAM comes standard? 3) How much RAM can be easily added? 4) How fast and what size is the hard drive? 5) Do you get one or two floppy drives? 6) What are the capabilities of the monitor/video controller combination? 7) What software comes with the package, and how useful is it to you?

MY RECOMMENDATIONS

If you want a computer strictly for business use, and your needs are modest, **and** you want to keep the cost down (or if you are a confirmed cheapskate), all you will need is a basic AT clone with a small (20MB-30MB) hard disk and a single floppy drive. The floppy drive should be a 5 1/4" rather than a 3 1/2". The reason for this is that the larger disks have been around longer, and there is more software available in 5 1/4" than 3 1/2". Make certain that the single disk drive will accept both DS/DD **and** DS/HD diskettes. The standard amount (640K) of RAM should be enough, and an EGA monitor should be sufficient for your needs. Whether or not you need a mouse will depend upon the software programs that you choose. If you choose a low end system such as this, be forewarned that you are quite likely to find yourself wanting a faster machine very soon.

Most people are far better advised to choose a system based on at least a 20Mhz 386SX processor. This will greatly improve performance on more complex tasks such as desktop publishing, computer graphics, management of larger databases and manipulation of larger spreadsheets. The minimum RAM you should consider is 2MB. **4MB is much better**. Your hard disk should be at least a 40MB. Better yet, 80MB. Consider getting two disk drives, one each 5 1/4" and 3 1/2" (high density), and a color VGA monitor.

Many people consider the 80386-25Mhz to be the best buy today. The reason for this is that a company called AMD has successfully cloned the Intel 80386 processor, and there is a sort of "chip war" (Remember the gas wars?) going on. On the other hand, the much more powerful 80486 is rapidly becoming the most popular processor for personal computers. If you go for either of these (386-25 or 486) be sure to get at least 4MB of RAM and at least a 65MB hard drive.

***** FLASH *****
As this edition goes to press, I have learned that a company called Cyrix has cloned the 80486. Look for prices to drop!
***** FLASH *****

Of course, if the computer in your future is a portable, you will have to consider all of the above factors, plus such things as size, weight and battery life.

Where to Buy

This is often a more difficult question than what to buy. Keep in mind that there is more to consider than just price. Guarantees and warranties can be very important. The minimum you should accept would be a full money back 90-day warrantee. It is not uncommon to see one-year, or even 18-month and two-year guarantees.

Another very important consideration for first-time buyers is technical support. Will the merchant (or manufacturer) be there for you after your check clears the bank? At least two of the major mail order firms (ZEOS and NORTHGATE) offer free, 24-hour-a-day, 365-day-a-year, toll free technical assistance.

Before you buy, find out where the nearest service representative is located. If you have a hardware problem, will you have to mail your system in, or will they send a representative to your site?

The main categories of computer merchants are as follows:

1. Stores that sell mostly computer stuff (computer stores).
2. Stores that sell computers and more (general merchandise).
3. Mail order sales.

Computer Stores

There are at least three different kinds of computer stores. **Brand name stores** sell brand name computers. This category includes national chains such as ComputerLand, MicroAge, Entre Computer Centers and Radio Shack, along with thousands of independently owned computer stores. **No name stores** often carry name brand peripherals, but they specialize in assembling computer systems right on-site from components purchased elsewhere. **Superstores** are giant stores that try to provide every computer thing you could possibly want under one roof. Included in this category are CompUSA and Micro Center.

Brandname Stores

Advantages

Good selection of brand names.
Prices, terms, warranties are all negotiable.

Disadvantages

Higher overhead costs must translate into higher consumer prices.

No-name Stores

Advantages

Low prices.
May use higher quality components.

Disadvantages

Unknown quality.
Unknown company stability.

Superstores

Advantages

Wide selection.
Prices lower than brand name stores.

Disadvantages

Not available in every location.
Less intimate compared to other stores.

General Merchandise Stores

Many stores sell computer equipment as a small part of their product line. Included in this classification are Sears, Kmart, Walmart, along with many lesser known retailers. Also in included are warehouse outlets such as Costco, Sam's Wholesale Club and Pace. Prices and conditions vary immensely from store to store in this category, so it is hard to nail down advantages and disadvantages for this type of merchant. One thing to keep in mind when shopping at a general merchandise store is that the salesman may or may not be knowledgeable.

Mail Order Sales

There are two types of mail order merchants. The first is a **warehouse outlet** that sells name brand computer products at a discount. The second type, called **proprietary mail order**, assemble computers and put their own name on them. Millions of dollars worth of computer equipment are bought and sold through the mail every year, usually to the satisfaction of the consumer. Every once in awhile someone gets burned. ***Always pay for a mail order purchase with a credit card.*** This offers you at least some protection.

Warehouse Outlet

Advantages

Wide selection.
Lowest prices.

Disadvantages

Buyer must pay shipping.
Usually no tech support.
Merchant may be too far away to hear complaints.

Proprietary Mail Order

Advantages

Low prices.
Tech support can be very good.

Disadvantages

Customer must pay shipping.
Often no on-site service.

Note. If you are leaning toward a system based on the 286 processor, consider this: you can probably find a comparable system, based on the 386SX for just a little bit more money (about $100 more). This will provide you with a very important option. If you really get into this computing stuff, and you decide to run Windows, or you want to enjoy multimedia, you will definitely wish that you had at least a 386SX.

Study the advertisements. Read only those articles evaluating PCs. Don't worry if you don't understand everything!

Be aware that in the computer world, things change rapidly. What was yesterday found on the high priced cutting edge is today found deep in the recesses of the bargain basement. Computer equipment depreciates rapidly, not from use, but rather from obsolescence. The good news is that this obsolescence won't affect your relationship with your computer. It might, however, tempt you to go out and buy the latest stuff.

Don't allow yourself to be intimidated. You now have enough information to make an informed decision. At some point in the future you may want to upgrade or go to an entirely different system, but for now, just try to remember this:

It is not so important which path you choose. The important thing is that you choose a path.

So, go forth and shop! Go get that PC.

Should you consider buying a used computer?

Used computers can offer the very best opportunities for obtaining maximum value for your dollar. Faster and faster technological developments cause computers to become "obsolete" sooner and sooner.

The fact is that these systems are not really "obsolete" at all. It would be more accurate to say that they are "not in vogue," or they are not "state-of-the-art." What they are is cheap, functional, and probably a very good deal.

However, if this is your first computer, I don't recommend buying a used computer. You will have no warranty, no service, and no technical support.

For some, the approach that makes the most sense is to start off with one of the less expensive new systems. Once you have learned your way around the ropes and have decided that computing is definitely for you, sell that system and shop around for exactly what you want on the used market.

Keep in mind when buying used that there is always the risk of buying someone else's problems. You should be generously rewarded for taking that risk by getting a rock-bottom price.

Commonly Asked Questions

Do I need a personal computer?

Absolutely not! It is entirely possible to lead a perfectly happy existence without one. You may be able to do some things much more efficiently with one, though. And when it comes to the competitive business arena, you **may** be severely handicapped without one.

What can a personal computer do for me?

A personal computer can balance your checkbook, act as your typewriter, serve as your editor, address your envelopes, entertain your kids, educate your kids, educate you, entertain you. It can figure your taxes, keep track of your Christmas card list, store your recipes, track your investments, draw pictures, and play music. You can use it to add and subtract, multiply and divide, or to remind you when the oil in the car needs to be changed.

When coupled with a modem, your personal computer can talk with other people, talk with other computers, listen to the stock market, take you shopping, reserve your airline tickets, and keep you informed of events around the world. It can access large libraries, plan your vacation, and even tell you whether or not to take your umbrella.

If you use your personal computer for business, it can process words, keep your books, control your inventory and project your costs. It can manage your mailing lists, sort your invoices, track your sales and oversee your accounts receivable. A personal computer can answer your phone, route your calls, and receive your FAXes. It can create invoices, letterhead and logos. You can use it to publish a company newsletter or to design your own advertising.

A personal computer can do all of this, and much, much, more.

How much does a personal computer cost?

Less this year than last year. Personal computers are a genuine bargain. Prices vary immensely, depending upon where you shop. ***As of this printing***, a basic 386SX system with 4MB RAM, color VGA monitor, graphics accelerator card, 100 MB hard drive, two floppy drives, keyboard, and 6 expansion slots cost between $1,400 and $2,300. Remember, price is only one consideration.

How do I know which system to buy?

You don't. You can't really know which system is right for you until you become a user, and you probably won't become a user until you buy your own system. As with other things in life, the first time you just have to trust someone. This could be a friend, someone at work, a computer salesman, or even me. If you decide to trust me, carefully read the chapter on Buying Your First PC.

Should I buy IBM, a clone, an Apple or a Mac?

Probably a clone. Why? Because IBM clones clearly offer the best value in personal computers. Also, there is more software available for IBM and compatibles than for Apples and Macs. To be fair, Apples and Macs have a devoted following as well, and they are favorites of Desktop Publishers, Engineers, and Graphic Artists. When in doubt, buy a clone.

Should I buy a new computer or a used computer?

Probably a new one. The best values are the used ones, but there are pitfalls and disadvantages, especially for the first time buyer. You might consider making an exception to this rule if the following conditions exist:

1. You get a warranty.
2. You know someone who will serve as your "tech support."
3. You can't afford a new computer.

After I buy my computer, what else do I need to buy?

Aside from the basic system (system unit, keyboard, and monitor) you will probably want a printer, unless this computer is only for playing games. You will also need some software. Hopefully, the most basic software, such as DOS and Windows, came with the system. (Check before you buy!) The software you need will depend upon the tasks you ask your computer to perform. Most people start out with word processing software, and add additional applications software as their confidence increases.

Do I need a mouse?

Whether or not you need a mouse depends upon the software that you buy. Some software do not require a mouse. Some software work much easier with a mouse, and some absolutely require a mouse. I recommend that you do get a mouse.

What kind of printer should I buy?

First decide whether or not you need an impact printer. If you do, the answer is simple: buy a dot matrix. If you don't need an impact printer, the choice is between an inkjet or a laser. Inkjets cost a little less, lasers are faster and more convenient.

How many disk drives do I need?

At least two. One hard and one floppy. Technically, you could get by with just one floppy, but unless you are looking at inexpensive portable computers, it makes no sense to omit the hard drive. Furthermore, the hard drive should store at least 40 megabytes.

Should I buy a computer that has a turbo?

"Turbo" simply means that you can slow the computer down if you need to. You will probably get one automatically.

How can I tell whether or not my computer will run a particular software package?

There are three primary things to consider. First, make certain that the software is designed for the platform you are using (IBM, Apple, etc.) Next, see if the software will work with the *version* of the operating system you are using. Then, make certain that your system has enough RAM to run the software. To be absolutely certain, call the software manufacturer. This should be an easy question for them to answer.

Should I spend big bucks for high-tech applications software, or should I buy inexpensive shareware?

That depends. For instance, if you write regularly, but have little interest in accounting, you might opt for the best word processing program that you can get your hands on, but you might send off for a $1.99 shareware program to help with your checkbook.

What is the single most important thing that I can do to make my transition into the computer world easier?

Find a Mentor. There is nothing like a real live human when it comes to explaining things. Your Mentor might be a friend, neighbor or someone at the office. If you are having trouble finding one, just join a computer club.

What is Multimedia?

MULTIMEDIA combines written and spoken words, still and moving pictures along with music and other sounds to convey an idea. Sometimes the computer does all of the work, generating as well as displaying the words, pictures etc. Sometimes the computer is used to control other equipment, such as slide projectors and stereo systems.

What do I need to upgrade to Multimedia?

First, you need to start off with at least a 386SX personal computer. If you have a 286 or less, and you want to enjoy multimedia computing, you need a new system. Special requirements are: stereo sound board, a fast CD-ROM drive, MS Windows (version 3.0 or later) and MS Windows Multimedia Extensions (included with Windows 3.1). The first two items on this list are hardware, the second two are software. In addition, a large hard disk (minimum 60MB) is recommended.

What is Virtual reality?

VIRTUAL REALITY uses a computer system to deliver sensory feedback, with the objective being to make the user feel as though she is somewhere else. Stereoscopic goggles provide the visual aspects, headphones the audio aspects, and special gloves and boots allow the computer to compensate for body movements.

Are there practical applications for virtual reality technology?

Yes. Aside from the obvious use for creating totally supercool video games, one practical application would be to allow an architect to stroll through a building to inspect it in its various stages of construction, before the first nail is driven.

Are there health hazards associated with computers?

Computers are pretty safe, especially when compared to other activities like crossing the street or breathing the air in major cities. There are a few things to keep in mind. There has been a continuing debate over the effect/non-effect of monitor radiation (electromagnetic radiation like that produced by your television). The fact is that no one ***really*** knows if your monitor (or television) is causing you any harm. Some people are concerned about this. Many are not. Those who are concerned should look for a monitor that meets the more stringent Swedish standards for shielding the user.

Some computer users report headaches that seem to be associated with computer use. Probable causes of this are muscle strain caused by prolonged sitting and eyestrain caused by glare on poorly lit screens. Remedies include frequent breaks to get up and move around and proper lighting on a freshly cleaned computer screen.

The monitor is not the only part of the computer that can cause you problems. Watch out for that keyboard, too! **REPETITIVE STRESS INJURY (RSI)** is an injury caused by doing the same thing hour after hour, day in and day out. In the case of computers, the most common area of the body to suffer is the wrist. To prevent possibly serious injury, use arm or wrist rests, and a good adjustable chair that puts you at a comfortable height.

Should I turn my computer off when I'm not using it, or should I leave it on all of the time?

While others will argue with me on this point, I say turn it off. Some argue that every time you turn the computer on, the wear and tear caused by the stress of having the components go from cold (room temperature) to hot (operating temperature) is far greater than the wear caused by leaving the computer running. On this point, they are probably correct. But that is not the whole story. What about the electricity that is being used to keep the machine going. True, it's not much, but it is continuous. Multiply that tiny amount by, oh, just say 100 million personal computers, and it starts to add up! Most importantly, though, is that I don't like to leave any electrical appliance turned on and unattended. What can I say? My dad was a fireman.

What about COMPUTER VIRUSES?

First of all, you can't catch a computer virus. A computer virus is just another computer program, but instead of being designed to make your life easier, it is designed to irritate and annoy you.

Computer viruses are spread in a number of ways. They can be transferred through infected floppy disks and they can be transmitted through unsafe telecommunications. They have even been known to show up on brand new systems, straight from the factory. The effects of a particular computer virus can range from rather harmless to totally destructive. Your computer won't explode or meltdown. In fact, the hardware will be unaffected. It is the software, or information that is damaged or destroyed.

There are antiviral programs that can be used to seek out and destroy computer viruses. Unfortunately, a newly developed virus might require a new antiviral program. So, before a new strain of virus can be countered, it first has to cause problems. Worse yet are the new **STEALTH VIRUSES**. These are diabolically designed to avoid detection and then destroy themselves after destroying your data, leaving not so much as a trace of their existence.

Other Reading

Computer Magazines

PC World
501 Second St. #600
San Francisco, CA 94107

PC Sources
PO Box 53298
Boulder, CO 80321-3298

PC Computing
PO Box 50253
Boulder, CO 80321-0253

PC Novice
PO Box 85380
Lincoln, NE 68501

Home Office Computing
PO Box 53561
Boulder, CO 80322-3561

PC Magazine
PO Box 51524
Boulder, CO 80321-1524

PC Home Journal
PO Box 469
Mt. Morris, IL 61054

PC Today
PO Box 85380
Lincoln, NE 68501

Books

The Beginner's Guide to Computers
Bradbeer, De Bono, Laurie
Addison-Wesley Publishing Company
©1982, 1989
ISBN 0-201-11209-4

A Computer Perspective
Charles & Ray Eames
Harvard University Press
©1973, 1990
ISBN 0-674-15626-9

The Devouring Fungus
Karla Jennings
W.W. Norton & Company
©1990
ISBN 0-393-02897-6

Computer Wimp No More
John Bear
Ten Speed Press
©1992
ISBN 0-89815-432-4

Introduction to Personal Computers
Katherine Murray
Que Corporation
©1990
ISBN 0-88022-539-4

Inside the IBM PC and PS/2
Peter Norton
Simon & Schuster, Inc.
©1990
ISBN 0-13-467317-4

On-Line Services

CompuServe
P.O. Box 20212
Columbus, OH 43220
(800) 848-8199

CompuServe offers access to over 1700 databases. Basic service includes information on news, weather and sports, up to 60 E-Mail messages, stock quotes, shopping and travel services, access to the *Grolier's Academic American Encyclopedia* and support for CompuServe. For more money, you get in-depth Financial Services (includes mutual funds and commodities), technical support (for computer hardware and software manufacturers), access to over 200 Forums, and the ability to use IQuest (CompuServe's gateway to extended research information, including many Dialog databases).

Dialog
3460 Hillview Ave.
Palo Alto, CA 94304
(800) 334-2564

Dialog specializes in providing research information to a wide variety of academic disciplines, including chemistry, engineering, social sciences, and humanities, through access to over 425 databases. They also offer CD-ROM subscription services and highly discounted (although limited access) after-hours use.

Prodigy
455 Hamilton Ave.
White Plains, NY 10601
(800) 776-0840

Prodigy is an IBM/Sears joint venture geared toward the home computer user. Services include shopping through the Sears catalog, home banking, E-mail, games, and forums. Prodigy also offers news, weather and sports information.

GEnie
401 N. Washington Street
Rockville, MD 20850
(800) 638-9636

GEnie, from General Electric, offers strictly text-based (no graphics) service at a lower rate than most other companies. Services include news and weather, shopping, software libraries, single and multi-player games, real time chat lines, and over 100 bulletin boards.

Dow Jones News
PO Box 300
Princeton, NJ 08540
(800) 832-1234

Dow Jones News specializes in business and financial news and information. Services include stock quotes, corporate information, up-to-the-minute world news, the complete *Wall Street Journal*, and articles from *Business Week, Forbes, Money Magazine, and Barron's.*

Dictionary of Terms

286
See Intel 80286

386
See Intel 80386

386SX
See Intel 80386SX

486
See Intel 80486

8086
See Intel 8086

8088
See Intel 8088

ABORT
A command for the computer to stop what it is doing, and standby for the next command.

ACCESS TIME
The period of time required by the computer to find a particular piece of information and retrieve it from its storage medium.

AMERICAN STANDARD CODE FOR INFORMATION INTERCHANGE
See ASCII.

APPLE
One of the companies that pioneered personal computers. Founded by two guys named Steve, Apple computers are known for their use of icons rather than typed commands, and their widespread use in the nation's schools.

APPLICATIONS SOFTWARE
Computer programs which allow the user to perform specific tasks, such as word processing, spreadsheet manipulations, and database management.

AREA NETWORK
See LOCAL AREA NETWORK.

ASCII
Pronounced "askee." Short for American Standard Code for Information Interchange. A standard binary code developed so all programmers would be using the same system.

ASYNCHRONOUS PORT
See SERIAL PORT.

AT
(Advanced Technology) A term coined by IBM for a particular computer design, and subsequently adopted by clone manufacturers.

BABBAGE, CHARLES (1791 - 1871)
Early pioneer of computer science. He devoted much of his life to the development of his "analytical engine," ultimately acknowledging that his concept was far ahead of the technology of the day.

BACKUP
To copy data in order to guard against unforeseen loss.

BAR CODE
An optically read binary code, such as found on merchandise in retail stores.

BASE MEMORY
The first 640K of RAM.

BASIC
Beginners' All-purpose Symbolic Instruction Code. A computer language which uses English-like statements, and ordinary mathematical notations.

BASIC INPUT/OUTPUT SYSTEM
See BIOS.

BAUD
A measure of the speed at which data is transferred. Often used (incorrectly) interchangeably with BPS.

BBS
Bulletin Board System. An electronic gathering place where users with common interests gather for information exchanges.

BIG BLUE
Nickname for IBM.

BINARY SYSTEM
A code which translates all letters, numbers, etc., into combinations of ones and zeroes.

BIOS
Basic input/output system. The computer programs which oversee the transfer of data between the CPU and other devices.

BIT
The smallest unit of information, as it appears to the computer. A bit is either a one or a zero.

BOARD
See PRINTED CIRCUIT BOARD.

BOOLEAN SEARCH
The ability of a database to search using the restrictions AND, OR, and NOT.

BOOT
A term which describes the automatic actions of a computer as it "comes to life." The term is derived from the act of a person lifting himself off the ground by pulling upwards on his own bootstraps.

BPS
Bits per second. A measure of the speed at which data is transferred. Similar, but not identical to BAUD.

BUFFER
Located in the computer's memory, a buffer is a temporary storage place for data.

BUG
The cause of a computer malfunction.

BYTE
A chunk of eight bits, used to represent a single number, letter, or other character.

CAD
Computer Aided Design. Software used to create mechanical drawings and other drafting products.

CAM
Computer Aided Manufacturing.

CD-ROM
A method of data storage whereby information is permanently stored on optically read disks. CDs can hold vast quantities of information.

CENTRAL PROCESSING UNIT
The brain of the computer.

CENTRALIZED NETWORK
See STAR NETWORK.

CENTRONICS PORT
See parallel port.

CGA
Color graphics adaptor. 320 x 200 pixels. Four different colors.

CHARACTER
One letter, number, or figure.

CHIP
See INTEGRATED CIRCUIT.

CIRCUIT BOARD
See PRINTED CIRCUIT BOARD.

CLIP ART
"Canned" graphics images on disk for use in desktop publishing.

CLOCK CHIP
A stable frequency source, used by the computer to keep the various components working together "in time."

CLOCK SPEED
A measure of the frequency of the computer's clock.

CLONE
A copy of an existing computer design.

CLOSED ARCHITECTURE
A type of computer design with no expansion slots, and therefore limited enhancement capability.

CMOS
Complementary Metal Oxide Semiconductor. Battery powered memory used to store the time, date and system configuration.

COBOL
Common Business-Oriented Language. A computer language specifically developed for business applications.

COLD BOOT
The boot which occurs when the computer is first turned on. See BOOT.

COMMAND
To instruct the computer to perform a specific action.

COMPATIBLE
A term used to describe computers which will operate the same software. Also used to refer to major brand hardware.

COMPUTER
An electronic machine capable of performing very simple tasks very rapidly.

COMPUTER LITERACY
A state of being fluent in computerese.

COMPUTER PROGRAM
A very specific, very explicit set of instructions which a computer can execute in order to perform a task.

COMPUTERESE
A special language spoken by users, power users, hackers and nerds.

CONTROLLER
An electronic device which supervises and serves to connect a particular peripheral with the CPU.

CONVENTIONAL MEMORY
See BASE MEMORY.

COPROCESSOR
An auxiliary brain which relieves the main processor of certain arithmetic tasks.

CP/M
Control Program/Microcomputers. A disk operating system, not compatible with MS DOS or PC DOS.

CPS
Characters Per Second. A measurement of printer speed.

CPU
See CENTRAL PROCESSING UNIT.

CRASH
A catastrophic failure.

CURSOR
The mark on the monitor which indicates where the computer will place the next character.

DAISY WHEEL
A noisy printer which closely resembles a typewriter, types letter quality text, but cannot do graphics.

DATA
Information.

DATA FRAME
In a serial interface, a unit of information which includes the eight bits that make up a byte, as well as additional bits that separate one byte from another.

DATABASE
A structured collection of related information.

DEBUG
Finding and fixing a computer malfunction.

DEFAULT
An automatic decision.

DELETE
To remove or erase.

DESKTOP PUBLISHING
The act of creating complex documents which integrate text, graphics, different styles of type, etc.

DEVICE
A general term for a piece of equipment which is attached to the computer.

DEVICE DRIVER
Software which expands DOS' capabilities and provides support for peripheral devices.

DIGITIZE
To convert information to binary codes.

DIP SWITCH
Tiny switches which can be set in order to configure a device to a particular system.

DIRECTORY
Similar to a table of contents, the directory provides a summary of the information on a disk, as well as a map of how to locate that information.

DISK
A storage device. See HARD DISK, FLOPPY DISK.

DISK DRIVE
Computer hardware which utilizes either floppy or hard disks.

DISK OPERATING SYSTEM
See DOS.

DISKETTE
Refers to floppy disk.

DISPLAY
The computer screen.

DOCKING STATION
A permanent chassis into which a portable computer can be plugged, expanding the system's capabilities.

DOCUMENT
A text file.

DOCUMENTATION
Computer lingo for written material such as an owners' manual or a reference manual.

DOS
Disk Operating System. A very basic computer program which allows the computer to obey your commands, and the commands of other software.

DOS PROMPT
The message displayed by DOS indicating it is awaiting your command.

DOS SALUTE
The act of simultaneously holding down the CONTROL and the ALT keys, and pressing the DELETE key. This action causes the computer to undergo a warm boot.

DOT MATRIX
A type of printer which utilizes pins to imprint tiny dots of ink onto the paper, can produce near letter quality text, and can also print graphics.

DOTS PER INCH
(DPI). A measure of the quality of print or graphics, as measured by the density of individual dots of ink.

DOUBLE SIDED/DOUBLE DENSITY
The "standard" version of a floppy disk.

DOUBLE SIDED/HIGH DENSITY
The "deluxe" version of a floppy disk.

DOWN
An inoperative state.

DOWNLOAD
To transfer information between computers.

DPI
See DOTS PER INCH.

DRIVER
See DEVICE DRIVER.

DS/HD
See DOUBLE SIDED/HIGH DENSITY.

DS/DD
See DOUBLE SIDED/DOUBLE DENSITY.

DUMP
The transfer of information from one place to another.

DVORAK KEYBOARD
A type of keyboard design which scrambles the position of the keys and scientifically places them according to their frequency of occurrence, as well as allowing for other factors, such as human anatomy. (I've never heard of anyone who actually uses a Dvorak keyboard.)

EGA
Enhanced graphics adaptor. 640 x 350 pixels. Sixteen different colors.

EISA
Extended industry standard architecture. The computer industry's response to IBM's MCA.

ELECTRONIC DISK
A portion of a computer's memory which is partitioned off from the rest, and acts like a very fast mechanical (floppy or hard) disk.

E-MAIL
Electronic Mail. An electronic system for sending, receiving and storing messages.

EMM
See EXPANDED MEMORY MANAGER.

EMULATION
The ability of one piece of hardware to behave like another.

ENIAC
(Electronic Numerical Integrator and Computer).
Early electronic computer (1946), developed at the University of Pennsylvania, using the then-available vacuum tube technology. ENIAC occupied 3,000 cubic feet and weighed 30 tons. Average time between vacuum tube failures: 7 minutes.

EPROM
Erasable Programmable Read-Only Memory. ROM which can be erased and changed.

ERROR
A message from the computer informing the user that a mistake has been made, and the user must figure out what that mistake was.

EXECUTE
To carry out instructions contained in a computer program.

EXPANDED MEMORY
Memory above 640K which is imported into base memory with the help of software called an Expanded Memory Manager.

EXPANDED MEMORY MANAGER
Software used to access RAM in excess of 640K.

EXPANSION BOARD
See Expansion Card.

EXPANSION CARD
A printed circuit board which plugs into an expansion slot, giving a computer additional capabilities.

EXPANSION SLOT
Sockets within the system unit into which circuit boards can be plugged in order to enhance the computer's capabilities.

EXPANSION PORT
Sockets, or "doors," on the back of the system unit, and used to connect peripheral devices to the computer.

EXTENDED INDUSTRY STANDARD ARCHITECTURE
See EISA.

EXTENDED MEMORY
Memory above 1 Meg available to DOS applications through a memory management program, when they are run in the processor's "protected mode," with a program like Windows.

EXTERNAL STORAGE
Secondary storage consisting of magnetic disks or tape.

FACSIMILE
See FAX

FAX
A system used for the transmission of images of documents over telephone lines.

FEAR
Anxiety caused by ignorance.

FIBRE OPTICS
Material used for the transmission of pulses of light. Future computers will no doubt rely on light pulses rather than electrical pulses.

FILE
An organized collection of related information, stored on a disk, with a unique name.

FIRMWARE
A term used for systems software permanently stored in ROM.

FIXED DISK
See HARD DISK.

FLOPPY DISK
A portable storage medium.

FONT
A complete collection of letters and other characters, all with the same typeface, and all the same size. Times Roman Italic 12 point, Times Roman Bold 11 point, and Times Roman Bold 14 point would be three separate fonts.

FORMAT
A command which tells the computer to create logical sectors on a disk, thus readying the disk to accept information.

FORTRAN
Formula Translator. A computer language widely used for scientific applications.

FUNCTION KEY
A button on the keyboard which, when pressed, causes a specific action to occur. Function keys are specific to individual software.

GARBAGE
Meaningless data.

GIGA-
Prefix for one billion.

GIGABYTE
1,073,741,824 (approximately one billion) bytes.

GIGO
Garbage In Garbage Out. A computer is only as good as its programmer.

GLITCH
A malfunction.

GRAPHICAL USER INTERFACE
A user friendly method of linking the computer operator with the hardware and software, via pictures rather than typed commands.

GRAPHICS
Computer generated drawings.

GUI
Pronounce "gooey." See GRAPHICAL USER INTERFACE.

HACKER
An amateur computer programmer or enthusiast.

HANDSHAKE
The successful "dialogue" of two devices.

HANDSHAKE LINES
In a parallel interface, wires which carry special messages that help ensure the computer and the peripheral device communicate successfully.

HARD DISK
A storage medium which is a permanent part of the computer, stores large amounts of information, and accesses that information very rapidly.

HARDWARE
If you can touch it, it's hardware.

HEAD
The portion of a disk drive which reads or writes information to or from a disk.

HELP
A special program designed to assist the user. Help programs are usually part of applications software.

HERCULES
A popular monochrome graphics adapter card.

HOST
See STAR NETWORK.

I/O PORTS
Input/output ports. See EXPANSION PORTS.

I/O
Input/Output.

IBM
The name of a company which is recognized as a leader in the development of personal computers.

ICON
A picture which is used to represent an idea.

INK JET
A nearly silent printer which sprays ink onto the paper, may be capable of printing multiple colors, and can be quite small.

INPUT DEVICE
Hardware whose function is to impart information to the computer.

INPUT/OUTPUT PORTS
See EXPANSION PORT.

INSTALL
To modify software for a particular computer.

INTEGRATED CIRCUIT
Tiny pieces of silicon onto which electronic circuits are formed.

INTEL
The primary manufacturer of CPUs.

INTEL 8086
A microprocessor capable of processing 16 bits of data internally, and connected to the rest of the computer with a 16 bit data path. This processor can only address one megabyte of RAM.

INTEL 8088
A microprocessor capable of processing 16 bits of data internally, but connected to the rest of the computer with an eight bit data path.

INTEL 80286
A microprocessor capable of processing 16 bits of data internally, and connected to the rest of the computer with a 16 bit data path. This processor can address up to 16 megabytes of RAM.

INTEL 80386
A microprocessor capable of processing 32 bits of data internally, and connected to the rest of the computer with a 32 bit data path. This processor can address up to four gigabytes of RAM. When teamed with software such as Windows, this processor enables multiple applications to run simultaneously.

INTEL 80386SX
Similar to the 80386, except that this processor is connected to the rest of the computer with a 16 bit data path.

INTEL 80486
Similar to the 80386, except that this processor can address up to 64 gigabytes of memory, and it has a built-in math coprocessor.

INTERFACE
The means by which the computer communicates with peripheral devices.

INTERNAL MEMORY
Primary storage consisting of silicon chips inside the computer.

JOYSTICK
A pointing device usually associated with computer games.

K
See KILOBYTE.

KB
See KILOBYTE.

KEYBOARD
Alpha-numeric input device.

KILO-
Prefix meaning one thousand.

KILOBYTE
1024 bytes.

KILOHERTZ
1000 cycles per second.

LAN
See LOCAL AREA NETWORK.

LAPTOP
A small, portable computer.

LASER PRINTER
A type of printer which uses laser technology to print high quality text and graphics swiftly and silently.

LCD
Liquid crystal display. Found on digital watches, pocket calculators, and some laptops.

LED
Light emitting diode, often used for indicator lights.

LEIBNIZ, Gottfried Wilhelm (1646-1716)
German mathematician who introduced the concept of "stepped reckoning," or the act of reducing a complex mathematical problem into many very simple problems.

LETTER QUALITY
A term for text which is of a quality suitable for business correspondence. Equal to that created on a typewriter.

LIMBAUGH, RUSH
The most famous E-mailbox holder in the world. Also happens to be right 98.4% of the time (documented), and works with talent on loan from God (undocumented).

LIM STANDARD
Software developed by Lotus, Intel and Microsoft to help DOS address memory above 640K.

LOAD
To copy information from storage and transfer it into RAM.

LOCAL AREA NETWORK
An array of computer equipment, located in a confined area such as a room or building. The equipment is interconnected by communication cables, allowing for the sharing of resources such as disk drives, printers, and software.

LOCAL NETWORK
See LOCAL AREA NETWORK.

LOOP
When the computer continues to do the same thing over and over again.

LUGGABLE
A transportable computer, bigger and heavier than a laptop.

M
See MEGABYTE.

MACINTOSH
An Apple manufactured computer.

MAINFRAME
A very large, very powerful computer.

MATH COPROCESSOR
See COPROCESSOR.

MAXI-SWITCH
A keyboard device which allows one to change the positions of the CAPS LOCK and the CONTROL keys.

MB
See MEGABYTE.

MCA
Micro Channel Architecture. A dramatic change made by IBM in 1987 to the design of their personal computers.

MEG
See MEGABYTE.

MEGA-
A prefix for one million.

MEGABYTE
1,048,576 (approximately one million) bytes.

MEGAHERTZ (Mhz)
A measure of the speed, or frequency, at which the CPU operates. Stands for millions of cycles per second.

MEMdisk
See ELECTRONIC DISK.

MEMORY RESIDENT PROGRAM
A program which continuously "runs in the background," until it is needed, and then returns to "stand-by" until called upon to perform again.

MEMORY
The primary storage devices containing the binary information that the computer needs for the job it is working on. See RAM, ROM, INTERNAL MEMORY.

MENU
A list of choices within a computer program.

MICRO CHANNEL ARCHITECTURE
See MCA.

MICROCOMPUTER
A small computer system such as a personal computer.

MICROPROCESSOR
See CENTRAL PROCESSING UNIT.

MICROSOFT
A software company, best known for the development of PC DOS and MS DOS, and most recently, Windows 3.1.

MIDI
Musical Instrument Digital Interface. Used for composing music with a computer.

MILLI-
Prefix meaning one thousandth.

MILLISECOND (ms)
A measure of the access time of a computer's disk drives, in thousandths of a second.

MINICOMPUTER
A medium sized computer larger than a PC and smaller than a mainframe.

MNP 4
A telecommunications standard concerning error detection between modems communicating at 2400 bps.

MNP 5
A telecommunications standard concerning data compression between modems communicating at 2400 bps.

MODEM
A device which is both an input and an output device, used to transmit and receive data over ordinary telephone lines.

MONITOR
The T.V. like device which allows the computer to communicate with the user.

MONOCHROME
Refers to single color monitors, most often green or amber.

MOTHERBOARD
The primary printed circuit board which ties together other important components.

MOUSE
A pointing device, used to facilitate rapid cursor movement.

ms
See Millisecond.

MS DOS
Microsoft Disk Operating System. See DOS.

MULTIMEDIA
Communication consisting of a combination of media including still and moving pictures, spoken and written word, music, etc.

MULTITASKING
The ability of an operating system to run more than one program simultaneously.

MUNCH
Two bytes.

NANO-
Prefix meaning one billionth.

NANOSECOND
A measure of the seek time of a computer's memory, in billionths of a second.

NEAR LETTER QUALITY
Describes print almost as good as that produced by a typewriter.

NERD
A male adolescent more interested in computers than baseball.

NERDETTE
A female adolescent more interested in computers than telephones.

NERDSTER
An adult nerd or nerdette.

NETWORK
A system of hardware and software which allows more than one computer to work together, usually devoted to a common function.

NLQ
See NEAR LETTER QUALITY.

NODE
In a network, each individual station.

NON-VOLATILE
Describes memory which does not rely upon a power supply to remain intact.

NOTEBOOK
A portable computer, smaller than a laptop, approximately the size of a small three-ring binder.

NYBBLE
Four bits, or one half of a byte.

OCR
See OPTICAL CHARACTER RECOGNITION.

OFFLINE
A condition of being functional, but not operating.

ONLINE
A condition of being functional and operating.

OPEN ARCHITECTURE
A type of computer design which allows for expansion, via expansion slots and expansion boards, and thus enabling the computer system to be easily enhanced.

OPERATING SYSTEM
Software which creates the environment in which the hardware, software, and operator interact. See DOS.

OPTICAL CHARACTER RECOGNITION
(OCR). The ability to scan and differentiate between characters such as letters and numbers. The computer actually "reads" rather than simply "copy."

ORPHAN
Refers to the first line of a paragraph when it appears alone at the bottom of a page.

OS/2
Operating System 2. Replaces PC-DOS on IBM's PS/2 computers. The primary advantage is that it does not suffer from DOS' 640K memory barrier. May have been rendered impotent by the introduction of Windows 3.x.

OUTPUT DEVICE
Hardware whose function is to display information to the user.

PARALLEL
A method of sending multiple bits of information simultaneously using multiple wires.

PARALLEL INTERFACE
The most common method of connection between a PC and a printer.

PARALLEL PORT
A socket used for connecting a peripheral device to the system unit. The device and the computer then communicate by sending information back and forth, one complete byte (8 bits) at a time.

PARK
A utility program which moves the read/write heads of the hard drive to a position where they will not damage the hard disk, should the system receive a sudden jolt.

PASCAL
A high-level computer programming language.

PASCAL, Blaise (1623-1662)
French scientist and inventor of an "arithmetic machine," capable of simple addition and subtraction.

PASSWORD
A code word used to restrict access to computer data.

PC
Sometimes this means simply "personal computer," and sometimes it refers to a particular model of IBM computer.

PC BOARD
See PRINTED CIRCUIT BOARD.

PC DOS
See DOS.

PCB
See PRINTED CIRCUIT BOARD.

PERIPHERAL
See PERIPHERAL DEVICE.

PERIPHERAL DEVICE
A device which attaches to the motherboard, enhancing the computer system's capabilities.

PERSONAL COMPUTER
A computer likely to be used by an individual or small business.

PIXEL
Short for "picture element," refers to each tiny dot of light that appears on the monitor.

PLAIN VANILLA
Refers to an unadorned, or unembellished state.

PLANAR BOARD
See MOTHERBOARD.

PLATFORM
Refers to the basic computer system being used. An IBM compatible with a 386 chip, color VGA monitor, 4 megabytes of RAM, and Windows 3.1 would be an example of a computing "platform."

PLATTER
One of the multiple disks of the hard disk.

PLOTTER
A printer like device used for high quality graphics products.

POINTING DEVICE
A peripheral device used to expedite cursor movement.

PORT
An electrical connection with the CPU, via the motherboard, in the form of a socket on the backside of the system unit.

POWER SUPPLY
An electronic component inside the system unit which converts the AC voltage of the supplied electricity to the correct DC voltage.

POWER USER
Someone who knows a lot about computers and how to get the most out of them.

PPM
Pages per minute. A measure of print speed.

PRINTED CIRCUIT BOARD
A plastic board with a network of thin interconnecting wires printed on its surface.

PRINTER PORT
See PARALLEL PORT.

PRINTER SPOOLER
A memory-resident program which stores information on its way to the printer, leaving the computer free to perform other tasks.

PRINTER
A peripheral device used for transferring information to sheets of paper.

PROCESSOR
See Central Processing Unit.

PROGRAM
See COMPUTER PROGRAM.

PROGRAMMER
One who writes computer programs.

PROMPT
A message from the computer asking for some form of input.

PROTECT
A term used to describe the act of securing a floppy disk so that it cannot be erased or written over.

PROTECTED MODE
A special operating mode for PCs running MS Windows which have at least a 80386SX processor, and at least 2 MB of RAM, allowing different programs to run simultaneously.

PS/1
IBMs latest introduction into the personal computer marketplace.

PS/2
The name coined by IBM for their second generation of computers, using a different design from the IBM PC series.

PUBLIC DOMAIN
A term for software which can be freely copied and used.

QUEUE
A "waiting room" for data which is to be processed.

QWERTY
A term describing the normal typewriter style of arranging the keys on a keyboard.

RAM
Random Access Memory is the "working memory" of the computer system.

RAMdisk
A portion of the computer's RAM which has been partitioned off and emulates a hard or floppy disk. See ELECTRONIC DISK.

RANDOM ACCESS MEMORY
See RAM.

READ
To detect stored information.

READ ONLY MEMORY
See ROM.

REAL TIME CLOCK
A battery powered device which allows the computer to keep track of the date and time.

RESET BUTTON
A button which, when pushed, causes the computer to undergo a warm boot.

RESOLUTION
Describes the clarity of the picture on the monitor.

REVERSE VIDEO
A feature on some monitors which allows the user to switch the color of the characters with the color of the background.

RGB
A color monitor which uses three separate electron guns, one for Red, one for Green and one for Blue.

ROM
Read Only Memory is memory permanently stored on microchips.

RS-232
See SERIAL INTERFACE.

RUN
To execute a computer program.

SAFETY
That peaceful feeling one feels when ignorance is replaced with knowledge.

SATELLITE
See STAR NETWORK.

SAVE
A term used to describe the act of copying information from RAM to a permanent storage medium.

SCANNER
An input device which digitizes graphical information.

SCROLL
To move the cursor up or down the screen.

SCSI
Small Computer System Interface. Pronounced "scuzzy." Similar to a very fast serial port.

SEEK TIME
The time required to find data stored in memory.

SEMI-CONDUCTOR
A term describing the electrical properties of elements such as silicon.

SERIAL
A method of sending multiple bits of information, single file, down the same wire.

SERIAL INTERFACE
A common method of connecting a PC and a peripheral device.

SERIAL PORT
A socket used for connecting a peripheral device to the system unit in a serial fashion.

SHAREWARE
Similar to Public Domain. Shareware authors request that users send them a donation.

SILICON
A common element used to make integrated circuits. Totally different from silicone.

SOCKET
An electrical connection into which an electronic component can be plugged.

SOFTWARE
Any set of instructions, or computer programs.

SPREADSHEET
Computer software designed to manipulate financial or statistical information, and answer "what if?" questions, by performing complex mathematical calculations.

STANDARD MEMORY
See BASE MEMORY.

STAR NETWORK
An array of computer equipment whereby one central computer acts as a "host" to lesser "satellite" terminals.

STORAGE DEVICE
Hardware whose function is to store information.

SURGE
An abrupt change in current or voltage.

SURGE SUPPRESSOR
A device placed between the power source and the computer to protect the computer against variations in voltage.

SYNTAX
Refers to the order or structure of a computer language.

SYSTEM BOARD
See MOTHERBOARD.

SYSTEM MEMORY
See BASE MEMORY.

SYSTEM UNIT
The main box of the computer. It contains components such as the motherboard, CPU, disk drives, power supply, and much more.

SYSTEMS SOFTWARE
Computer programs which give the computer sufficient instructions to get itself up and running, and to maintain itself.

TECHNOLUST
A modern day gluttony marked by an insatiable appetite for every technological gadget available.

TERMINAL
See NODE.

TEXT
Words and numbers, as opposed to drawings (graphics).

TOGGLE KEY
A keyboard button which, when pressed, activates a particular feature and, when pressed a second time, deactivates that same feature.

TONER
Material used by laser printers instead of ink.

TRACKBALL
A stationary pointing device.

TSR
Terminate and Stay Resident. See MEMORY RESIDENT PROGRAM.

TTL
Transistor-Transistor Logic. A type of monitor.

TURBO
Describes a microprocessor capable of operating at two speeds.

TWO GUYS NAMED STEVE
Developers of the first true home computer.

UNINTERRUPTED POWER SUPPLY
A power source independent of the normal power grid.

UNIVAC
Early electronic computer, introduced by Remington Rand in 1951. UNIVAC was the first computer capable of processing both numbers and letters.

UNIX
An operating system, developed by AT&T, and found on larger computers.

UPLOAD
To receive information from another computer.

USER FRIENDLY
A term used to describe aspects of computing which require minimum specialized knowledge.

USER
Any person who directly utilizes a computer.

UTILITY PROGRAM
Subroutines of DOS which aid in disk and file management.

V.32
A telecommunication standard that defines how modems connect to each other when communicating at 9600 bps.

V.32bis
A telecommunication standard that defines how modems connect to each other when communicating at 14,400 bps.

V.42
A telecommunication standard that controls point-to-point error control.

V.42bis
A telecommunication standard that defines how modems compress data sent between them.

Vdisk
See RAMDISK.

VDT
Video display terminal. See MONITOR.

VERSION
Just as books may have a second or third edition, software may have different versions.

VGA
Video graphics array. 640 X 480 pixels. 256 different colors.

VIDEO CONTROLLER
Hardware inside the system unit specifically matched to the monitor.

VIRTUALdisk
See RAMDISK.

VIRTUAL REALITY
Once a science fiction idea, now a real life technology that creates a separate reality and projects it upon our senses using special helmets, gloves, etc.

VIRUS
A program designed with malice and forethought to cause harm and destruction to computer data.

VOLATILE
Describes memory which is erased when the power to it is removed.

WAIT STATE
When a computer's memory outperforms the other components, it is necessary for the memory to pause and allow the computer to catch up. If the rest of the computer is capable of keeping up with the memory, the computer will have "zero wait states."

WARM BOOT
Any boot performed after the computer has been turned on. See BOOT.

WIDOW
Refers to the last line of a paragraph when it appears alone at the top of a page.

WINCHESTER
See HARD DISK.

WINDOWS
A powerful, multi-tasking, graphical user interface for DOS-based systems.

WIZARD
An expert computer programmer.

WORD PROCESSING
The process of computer aided text creation and manipulation.

WORM
Write **O**nce **R**ead **M**any. Refers to CD ROM technology, expanded to allow one-time writing to the disk.

WRAP AROUND
A word processing feature which causes the text to automatically shift down to the next line after the right margin has been reached.

WRITE
To record information on some storage medium.

WRITE-PROTECT TAB
A sticky paper tab which can be affixed to a floppy disk to prevent it from being written on or erased.

WYSIWYG
What You See Is What You Get. A term used to describe the desirable situation that exists when the screen accurately portrays the image of a full page of a document. Pronounced "wizzy-wig."

XENIX
An operating system similar to UNIX, developed by Microsoft Corporation, for use on personal computers.

XT
A term coined by IBM for a particular model computer, and subsequently used by clone manufacturers. Derived from the term "extended technology."

Index

Colophon

This book was written in WordPerfect on a Northgate Slimline 320, which uses an Intel 80386 microprocessor, running at 20 Mhz. Graphics were scanned with a Logitech ScanMan hand scanner. Pages were printed on a Hewlett Packard LaserJet IIP. The cover was printed on a Varityper 4200B-P high resolution imagesetter at 1800 dpi.

Body text is New Century Schoolbook and headings are Helvetica. Dictionary and Index are Helvetica. All are from Pacific Data Products' Pacific Page cartridge.

The printer was McNaughton & Gunn.

The only thing more expensive than education is ignorance.

Benjamin Franklin

Order Form

Is someone you love missing out on the JOYS OF COMPUTING? Why not get them their very own copy of *COMPUTER ANXIETY? Instant Relief!*

Please send me ____ copies of ***COMPUTER ANXIETY? Instant Relief!*** I enclose $9.95 for each book, plus $2.05 for shipping Book Rate, **or** $4.05 for shipping Air Mail.

(quantity discounts available)

Total cost, including shipping:

$12.00 Book Rate	(allow 3-4 weeks for delivery)
$14.00 Air Mail	(allow 3-4 ***days*** for delivery)

Name: ______________________________

Address: ______________________________

City: ______________________________

State: ____________________ Zip Code: ____________

Mail to:

CASTLE MOUNTAIN PRESS
P.O. BOX 190913
ANCHORAGE, AK 99519-0913
(907) 563-6166